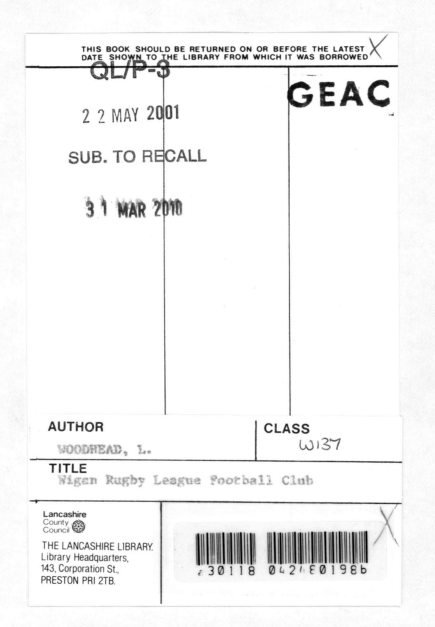

1. Cup of joy! Eric Ashton shows his delight as he holds the most famous Rugby League prize of all after the 1959 Challenge Cup final triumph against Hull.

2. Wigan captain Graeme West and his team-mates with the Lancashire Cup after the 1986 victory against Oldham at St Helens.

Wigan Rugby League Football Club

3. Remember them? A team packed with famous names from the 1955-56 season. *back row, left to right:* McGurrin, Bretherton, Hayward, Mather, Cherrington, Griffin, Bird, Bolton. *front:* Boston, Chisnall, Broome, Ashcroft, Cunliffe, Parr.

First published 1989 by
Archive Publications Ltd
10 Seymour Court
Manor Park
Runcorn
Cheshire
WA7 1SY

in association with

The Liverpool Daily Post & Echo Ltd
PO Box 48
Old Hall Street
Liverpool L69 3EB

ISBN: 0-948946-63-6

4. Talented stand-off Dave Bolton in a typical break for Wigan. In this flashback to 1959 he is being challenged by Hull fullback Colin Hutton.

Introduction

Leslie Woodhead is Deputy Editor of the *Liverpool Echo* and has been its Rugby League writer for more than twenty years.

He writes with knowledge and a deep-rooted affection for the game, having followed it and recorded it at every level from junior football through to the top international occasions and Wembley finals.

He admits to being hooked on Rugby League football from a very early age, and says that, for him, it has never lost its magical appeal!

The game of Rugby League football, played at its best, is one of the finest sporting spectacles in the world. It is a game of spectacular action, breathtaking excitement, superb athletic achievement . . . and marvellous entertainment!

I have had the pleasure of following the sport for as long as I can remember. Early days of being taken as a small boy to Wilderspool to watch some great Warrington sides in action developed into a much wider sphere of interest in Rugby League football in general.

Later the opportunity came along to write about the sport and that breadth of interest — and enthusiasm — widened still further.

Rugby League is that kind of entertainment. It readily captures the imagination and, to its everlasting credit, it has immense appeal to every member of the family.

It is also a sport which has produced many great clubs with famous sides rich in talent, and when you look at all those great qualities the name of Wigan is inevitably among those which come to mind. Over the years they have established themselves time and time again as world leaders and world beaters.

When I started to delve into their history for this book it became a fascinating journey of sheer Rugby League delight, tracing the Wigan story from its humble beginnings and on through some of the most memorable events in the game's history.

The preparation, the writing and the many hours spent sorting through the picture files evoked countless memories of memorable games and great players. I hope that the reader experiences the same amount of enjoyment from this tribute to a great Rugby League club.

Special thanks must go to all those talented photographers who so skilfully recorded the events covered in these pages.

Leslie Woodhead

Contents

The name of Wigan is synonymous with all that is best in the great game of Rugby League football. Over the years the Central Park club has achieved records of success, set standards of excellence and attracted levels of support which countless others have strived to emulate.

The huge honours board outside the Wigan ground — regarded by many as the real home of Rugby League — bears proud testimony to the many great trophy-winning occasions in the club's history. It is a history interwoven with a glittering silver thread, reflecting more cup triumphs than any other club in the game. Wigan have established the kind of record which, way back in the Fifties, inspired their supporters to coin the phrase: "Show Wigan a cup and it's theirs!"

Those trophy achievements, the years of Wembley glory, the countless personalities who have worn the famous cherry and white shirt, the enterprise, the progress — on and off the field — and the high entertainment factor weave their way through the Wigan story. They have helped make Wigan Rugby League Football Club just as famous a world landmark as the town's legendary Pier!

World leaders and world beaters! Wigan have earned those accolades many times over the years. Just look at their record:

• They have been Champions of the Rugby League no fewer than nine times — plus First Division Champions and League Leaders' Trophy winners. Even Adolph Hitler could not stop Wigan from winning trophies — they were kingpins of the emergency wartime competition in the 1943-44 season as well!

• The Rugby League Challenge Cup first had the cherry and white ribbons fluttering from it as far back as 1924. Since then Wigan have had their name engraved on that handsome piece of RL silverware ten times and have been finalists on nine other occasions.

• Every one of the game's top awards has been carried back in pride to Wigan at some time or another: Lancashire League nineteen times, including the Lancashire War League; Lancashire Cup on twenty occasions; John Player Trophy a record four times; Premiership, Charity Shield twice; and the old BBC2 Floodlit Trophy.

• Wigan have appeared in more Challenge Cup finals (nineteen) than any other club, and their players have also brought many great individual honours and records to the club from both sides of the world.

From the very early days of Rugby League football Wigan have always had a reputation for signing players of exceptional quality. The star names, the great personalities and the outstanding crowd-drawing stars who have become household names throughout the game would fill volume upon volume in their own right.

Wigan's Hall of Fame of outstanding Rugby League talent would go on and on. It is not possible to spotlight them all, but here is just a brief sample of some of the all-time greats who have worn the cherry and white. It will jog a few memories — and remember there are countless other top players who also qualify for the list.

Names include Jim Leytham, a leading try scorer from the early years of the century, and Johnny Ring, rated as one of the greatest wingers ever to grace the game. Also Brian Nordgren, Cec Mountford, Ken Gee, Joe Egan, Tommy Bradshaw, Martin Ryan, Johnny Lawrenson, Brian McTigue, Billy Boston, Eric Ashton, Dave Bolton, Fred

Griffiths, Ellery Hanley, Andy Gregory, Graeme West etc . . . the list is endless of names which conjure up a million great memories. There are famous partnerships, too, like Ashton and Boston, who were one of the greatest wing partnerships of all time.

When talking about all-time greats one name is inevitably boldly emblazoned on that list: Jim Sullivan.

When Jim Sullivan steered home no fewer than twenty-two goals in a Challenge Cup match against amateur side Flimby and Fothergill in February 1925 he created a record for goals in one match which has stood the test of time and the challenge of many other brilliant goalkickers right to this day. The mighty 'Sully' also set up the best ever total of goals in a career with his incredible haul of 2,867 between 1921 and 1946.

Jim Sullivan became more than a name in the Rugby League game. He was a legend! He had come up from the Welsh valleys at the age of just seventeen in 1921, with Wigan pipping Wakefield Trinity for his signature. Sully chose Wigan and started a career which became a milestone in the game's history. He served the Central Park club, Wales and Great Britain with outstanding distinction. His most prolific scoring season was 1933-34 when he hit the goal target two hundred times.

5. Johnny Ring, one of Wigan's most famous wing stars — and there have been many outstanding wingmen at Central Park over the years. Ring played for Wigan between 1922 and 1932 during which time he scored 371 tries including a record-breaking season when he touched down no fewer than 61 times.

Sully toured Down Under to Australia and New Zealand three times, in 1924, 1928 and 1932, when he captained the British side. All his football over a quarter of a century was with Wigan, apart from a short wartime spell, and he established himself as the game's greatest fullback and most successful goalkicker on record. Before Jim Sullivan finally hung up his boots he had played no fewer than 928 games.

Sullivan's story could occupy an entire volume in its own right. The great man's record underlines the tremendous impact he made on Rugby League football. He was forty-two when he played his final game in 1946 and Wigan fans still mention his name with a special pride. In no fewer than eighteen successive seasons up to the start of the war Jim Sullivan's powerful precision kicking brought him centuries of goals. He earned every one of the game's top honours as well as captaining Wigan and the international sides.

It was Jim Sullivan who first held Rugby League's most glittering prize aloft at Wembley when the game's greatest showpiece occasion — the Challenge Cup final — was first staged at the famous stadium. That was in 1929, but Wigan had already firmly engraved their name in cup and league football long before then.

Humble Beginnings

The club had its humble beginnings in 1879 at a ground in Dicconson Street where it paid the princely sum of £2 10s in rent — per season! It moved to Prescott Street in 1886 and three years later the first of that never-ending sequence of trophies went back to the Lancashire town: it was the West Lancashire Cup — a major prize in those days — and Wigan won it by beating Aspull in the final at St Helens. Wigan have been winning trophies with impressive regularity ever since!

In the late 1800s a more serious issue dominated the sport when allegations concerning professionalism and under-the-counter payments rocked the Rugby world. The seeds of the Northern Union were being sown. Open professionalism was on its way, and when the historic break came Wigan were among the pioneers of the new organisation. Their first professional season produced receipts of £556 as attendances began to increase; this was a staggering sum then, and is even more staggering in comparison to today's golden gates!

Wigan, though, were soon home-hunting again, and they spent a season at Springfield Park, home of the soccer club, for the first time breaking the £1,000 barrier in total gate receipts for a season and also winning the Lancashire Senior Competition despite strong rivalry from Widnes. Then in 1902 Wigan made one of the most momentous moves in the club's history: the Central Park legend was about to be born . . .

On a cold January evening the Rugby League die-hards of the town gathered for a meeting in the Public Hall in King Street where they decided that Wigan would have a new ground. The venue would be Powell Street, and on 6

6. The great Jim Sullivan in typical goalkicking action. He became a legend in the game — one of Rugby League's all-time greats — and his record of 22 goals in one match still stands to this day.

September 1902 Wigan played their first match there to set the ball rolling on a Rugby League legend: Central Park, a name which has become respected and admired wherever Rugby League football is a talking point. And that famous ground has provided plenty to talk about over the years. It has been graced by some of the finest players and most memorable teams in the world and it has seen excitement, high drama and football so outstandingly skilful as to provide a lifetime of memories for millions of Rugby League followers. All from those humble beginnings.

The opening of a new ground these days would call for a match with a World XIII, a derby clash with traditional rivals St Helens, a game against Australia's best or some other side of outstanding attainment. When Wigan first took the field at Central Park all those years ago the visitors for the big occasion were Batley, then one of the powers in the game.

Wigan gave a foretaste of things to come with their first victory on home soil by 14-8. The men who scored the first of countless points to follow over the years were J Barr, who made history with Central Park's opening try, and Dicky Rothwell, who kicked the first goal on the ground.

The cash began to flow. That first season at the new ground produced receipts of just over £3,000. The following season the figure leaped to £4,467. Wigan were really on their way! And if supporters think that the big-crowd atmosphere was something which did not arrive on the Wigan scene until the Thirties, they are mistaken — 30,000 times over — because that was the attendance which packed Central Park one afternoon in November 1907 for the first tour game at the ground. Receipts were £1,500.

New Zealand were the visitors, Wigan won 12-8 and the teams for that historic game lined up like this: Wigan consisted of Sharrock, Leytham, Jenkins, T Thomas, Miller, J Thomas, Battersby, Cheetham, Silcock, Blears, Brooks, Wilcock, Ramsdale; and the New Zealand team was made up of Turtill, Messenger, Rowe, Wrigley, Smith, Todd, Wynward, Wright, Tyler, Cross, Lile, Pearce, Byrne.

These were the early days of the big crowds . . . and early days for sponsorship, too. Not the big-money sponsorship which nowadays pours thousands of pounds into the game each season, but a novel method of rewarding exceptional playing feats. The first recorded example of sponsorship in the Rugby League game could well have been in 1912 when a firm of Wigan outfitters promised a special prize for every player scoring three tries in one match. From what I can glean from those early records, four players — Todd, Bradley, Ramsdale and Curran — each scored a hat trick in one game and qualified for the prize . . . a new overcoat!

Even in those days Wigan were establishing a reputation of success in the Lancashire Cup. They first won the trophy in 1905 (after a replay) and went on to triumph in the competition on six more occasions up to the outbreak of the Second World War. They were also beaten finalists eight times during that period.

The Big One — the Northern Union Challenge Cup, later to become the Rugby League Challenge Cup — proved an elusive prize for the men of the famous cherry and white until 1924. They had reached the final for the first time in 1911 with a team which was hailed as one of the best since the club's formation. This was their final line-up: Sharrock, Leytham, Jenkins, Todd, Miller, Thomas, Cleave, Ramsdale, Whittaker, Cheetham, Silcock, Williams and Seeling.

Wigan were red-hot favourites to win. They had set the cup tie fever running through the town with some outstanding wins on their way to the final against some of the strongest teams in the competition — Huddersfield, Warrington, Leeds and Batley. Now they were due to take on Broughton Rangers in the final at Salford, but the ground was in such a bad state after continuous and heavy rain that the Wigan committee, upon seeing the playing area, immediately objected to the match going ahead. Three members of the old Northern Union Committee were there and went into hurried session to make a decision. They ruled against Wigan and the game went ahead.

The appalling day kept the crowd down to just 8,000, the lowest in the history of the cup, with receipts of just £376! It was a gloomy day all round for the Wigan supporters who travelled to Manchester and saw their team beaten 4-0 with two goals by Scott. Wigan rarely looked like scoring throughout the whole match.

The hopes of the Wigan supporters for that big silver 'pot' were again carried high as they made the long journey across the Pennines for their next Challenge Cup final, this time against mighty Huddersfield at Leeds in 1920. But it was disappointment again — Huddersfield won 21-10 before a crowd of 14,000.

The crowds who stood on the Central Park terraces had seen their team win the Lancashire Cup and carry off the Championship, but the one they really longed for continued to elude them. The year after the Cup final defeat against Huddersfield they were knocked out in the first round against St Helens Recs. But hopes rose in the two following seasons as Wigan moved impressively into semi-finals, only to lose each time to Hull.

Then season 1923-24 dawned with optimism running high and the Wigan faithfuls hoping that it was surely *their* year for the Big One.

That hope burned brightly as Wigan began to pick up their old cup routine, moving through the rounds with good wins, beating Leigh 7-5 at home, then hammering Broughton Rangers 49-0 before travelling to Hunslet where they triumphed 13-8. They were back in the semi-finals for the third successive year — would it be third time lucky?

Thousands of Wigan supporters headed for Salford for the match with Barrow to decide who went through to the final. Wigan left nobody in any doubts as they raced to a 30-5 victory.

Wigan were back in the final, but this was still before the heady days of Wembley and that magical trip south. In its own way, though, the big match still carried a lot of glamour in the northern working class setting of Rochdale.

Oldham were another great Rugby power of the time and they had also won their way through to the game's most prestigious occasion. The roads around the Rochdale ground were choked with supporters as a crowd of 41,831 made their way to the final. They poured out receipts of £3,712, and although both figures are small beer in comparison to the 95,000 Cup final attendances of recent years and gates topping the million pounds mark, back in 1924 that crowd figure at Rochdale was a record for any professional Rugby match in the country up to that time.

So many people wanted to see the final that hundreds spilled inside the railings around the field of play and stood around the edges of the pitch. Mounted police had to be called in to keep the fans from encroaching onto the pitch, and when the famous South African winger, Van Heerden, went over for a try he also had to run around a mounted policeman over the line before touching down!

The referee for the match that day was Frank Chambers, a Congregational minister. Playing at scrum half for Oldham was George Hesketh, a former Wigan player who later rejoined the Central Park club as a board member and eventually became chairman.

Wigan fielded the following team: Sullivan, Ring, Howley, Parker, Van Heerden, Hurcombe, Jerram, Webster, H Banks, Brown, Roffey, Van Rooyen and Price, who was reputed to be the fastest forward in the game at that time. Eight of the players had come up from Wales and Van Rooyen, the famous South African forward, went on to earn another Cup final winner's medal with Widnes six years later.

Wigan outclassed Oldham in the final, winning 21-4, and when the team returned home people turned out in their thousands to give them the kind of welcome which had never before been seen in the Lancashire town.

Wigan's success story, though, had not been confined to the cup competitions and league championships. They had also distinguished themselves against some of the greatest teams in the world — the touring Australians and New Zealanders. When the Aussies came to Lancashire in October 1911 it was Wigan who gave them their first defeat of the tour with a 7-2 victory in front of 25,000 spectators.

7. The way it was . . . action at Central Park in October 1936.

8. Cec Mountford, that fine New Zealand stand-off, shows his distribution skills as he slips the ball away from a tackle by De Lloyd during the top four clash with Warrington at a packed Central Park in November 1946.
9. A Wigan line-up from March 1948.

Wembley

In the Twenties the date which stands out above all others in the Wigan calendar, and which provides a major milestone in the history of Rugby League football in general, was Saturday 4 May 1929.

In an effort to popularise the game in the south, and London in particular, league officials had decided to switch the final of the Rugby League Challenge Cup to Wembley Stadium for the first time. And when history is made you can bet that Wigan are there or thereabouts. In 1929 it was Wigan and Dewsbury players who made that historic walk down the Wembley tunnel to act as pioneers for the game at the Stadium.

The two teams started a tradition which has become the high spot of the game's calendar, and those 45,000 spectators who made the long, trying journey south were forerunners of the millions who have made the annual pilgrimage for Rugby League's most glittering showpiece occasion of the year.

Jim Sullivan led out the Wigan side which lined up like this: Sullivan, Brown, Kinnear, Parker, Ring, Abram, Binks, Hodder, Bennett, Beetham, Stephens, Mason and Sherrington. It was Sullivan who led the way to the Royal stand at the end of the match to receive the trophy from Lord Daresbury after his team had beaten the Yorkshiremen 13-2. Sullivan, the first man to receive the Cup at Wembley, was also the first Rugby League player to score there with an early goal. The honour of the opening Wembley try went to Syd Abram (who was later to become a referee).

Victory completed a tough and testing Cup campaign for the cherry and whites who had to survive two replays against St Helens sides, first beating the Saints in the third round replay at Central Park, then triumphing over St Helens Recs by 13-12 in the replay at Leigh after a 7-7 semi-final draw at Swinton.

Wigan continued to dominate the league and carried off the Championship in 1934 when they beat Salford 15-3 in the final at Warrington, but the war clouds were gathering over Europe and the outbreak of the Second World War plunged Rugby League, like every other sport, into disruption.

An emergency competition helped to provide welcome relief in the way of sporting entertainment for those on the home front during the difficult war years, and Wigan raised the spirits of wartime Wiganners with some good displays, including success in the 1943-44 Emergency Wartime Championships, beating Dewsbury with a 25-14 aggregate in a final played over two legs.

When the war ended and Rugby League began to get back to normal with players returning from the Forces, Wigan were soon into their trophy-winning stride again to give their loyal followers something to cheer about in those austere years immediately after the war.

More than 28,000 people poured into Wilderspool Stadium at Warrington in 1946 to see Wigan take on Widnes in the final of the Lancashire Cup — a record crowd for the Warrington ground. Wigan, finalists for the sixteenth time, looked to be on their way to their eighth win in the competition, but with just ten minutes left Tommy McCue, the famous Widnes scrum half and a master in the art of tactical kicking, placed one of his perfectly-judged grubber kicks to the posts, and before Wigan could make the danger safe in came Reynolds to swoop for the touchdown. Hutton added the goal, followed by a drop goal soon after, and Widnes had won 7-3.

There was still the Challenge Cup to come and a chance for Wigan followers to return to Wembley for the first time since that inaugural final of 1929.

London was still bearing scars of the blitz as the charabancs and steam trains rolled into the capital from the north in May 1946 to see Wigan take on Wakefield Trinity.

The cherry and whites were without four of their stars who were on their way along with the Great Britain team for the tour of Australia — Ted Ward, Martin Ryan, Ken Gee and Joe Egan. Then, on the morning of the match, there were fears that Wigan would have to make a late and dramatic team change: Jack Cunliffe, who was to play at fullback, had been taken ill during the night. As it turned out no change was needed but the story at the time said that if Cunliffe had been forced to drop out, Wigan's trainer-coach Jim Sullivan, who had played his final match for the club two months previously at the age of forty-two, would have made a dramatic return to the team — almost seventeen years after leading Wigan in their first Wembley final!

This is how Wigan finally lined up: Cunliffe, Nordgren, Ashcroft, Ratcliffe, Jolley, Lowrey, Bradshaw, Banks, J Blan, Barton, Watkins, Atkinson and W Blan.

The day before the game Jack Blan, who had been called in to take the hooking role in the absence of Joe Egan, said that he had been dreaming about diving over for tries at Wembley — and in fact he did go on to score two tries! Jolley and Nordgren also scored, but Wigan lost in the most dramatic circumstances with Billy Stott kicking a penalty for Wakefield with just minutes left to play to give the Yorkshiremen a 13-12 victory.

Wigan supporters went home disappointed but still turned out in their thousands to give their team a heroes' welcome home — and just a couple of weeks later those loyal supporters had their reward when Wigan carried off the Rugby League Championship, beating Huddersfield 13-4.

It was the custom then — a trend which has returned in recent seasons — to stage major Rugby League finals on soccer club grounds and the Wigan-Huddersfield title decider was held at Maine Road, home of Manchester City FC, where a crowd of 67,136 poured through the turnstiles.

A clever blind-side break from the scrum by Tommy Bradshaw in the second half sent fullback Jack Cunliffe over for a try which proved the turning point of the final after Wigan had been holding a tenuous 5-4 lead.

Wigan's team on that memorable day was: Cunliffe, Nordgren, Ratcliffe, Ashcroft, Jolley, Lowrey, Bradshaw, Banks, J Blan, Barton, Atkinson, Watkins and W Blan.

Exactly twelve months later Wigan players were stepping out at Maine Road again, this time to face Dewsbury in the Championship final.

10. Wembley bound. Wigan players, wearing their new black blazers with facings in the club colours of cherry and white, line up at Wigan Station before leaving for the 1948 Cup final against Bradford Northern.

Fullback Jim Ledgard gave the Yorkshiremen an early lead with a penalty goal but Wigan stormed back with a try by their New Zealand wing star Brian Nordgren, leading the way to a memorable 13-4 victory. Wigan's winning line-up was: Cunliffe, Nordgren, Ward, Ashcroft, Lawrenson, Mountford, Bradshaw, Gee, Egan, Banks, Barton, W Blan and J Blan.

It was a historic moment for the team when they received the trophy for the sixth time — an achievement which no other club in the game could match. It was the perfect crowning touch to a truly memorable season which had also seen Wigan winning the Lancashire Cup with a 9-3 win in the final at Swinton against Belle Vue Rangers, the Manchester-based club. That was a triumph which started a magnificent sequence of success in the county competition with Wigan reeling off six successive years of Lancashire Cup victories, beating Belle Vue Rangers once again, as well as Warrington (twice) and Leigh (twice) in the finals to become undisputed Kings of the County Cup. Then in the 1949 final against Leigh at Warrington Brian Nordgren raced in for a record haul of four tries — a record which still stands supreme to this day.

But Wembley still remained the glittering prize, and the Wigan folk who stood on the Central Park terraces every Saturday afternoon to give their team some of the strongest support in the game did not have to wait long to go "Up for the Cup" again.

Memories of the 1946 disappointment must have still been in the minds of many of those Wiganners who travelled south in May 1948 to see their team take on Bradford Northern. No fewer than 91,465 people poured into Wembley Stadium, the biggest Cup final crowd up to that date.

Both teams included a host of famous names. Wigan fielded Ryan, Ratcliffe, Ward, Ashcroft, Hilton, Mountford, Bradshaw, Gee, Egan, Barton, White, Blan and Hudson. Bradford Northern fielded Leake, Batten, Case, Ernest Ward, Edwards, Davies, D Ward, Whitcombe, Darlison, Smith, Tyler, Foser and Traill.

The final not only brought together two great sides: it was also auspicious for being the first Rugby League Challenge Cup final attended by Royalty. King George VI and Queen Elizabeth were the Chief Guests.

Wigan opened well with a try by Jack Hilton after twenty minutes. Ted Ward kicked the goal but Northern hit back quickly with winger Alan Edwards going over for a try, making it 5-3 at half time. Wigan eventually crowned their win in the second half when prop Frank Barton snapped up a try in the closing minutes.

When Joe Egan and his men travelled back to their home town with the Cup a massive welcome awaited them. From the moment their train passed through Warrington it seemed that just about every railway embankment was lined with cheering, waving supporters.

But that was nothing compared to the scenes in Wigan where 100,000 people turned out to greet their heroes. As the Wigan players stepped off the train the station announcer called out "Hearty congratulations to the Wigan team from the station master and his staff!" A band on a motor lorry preceded the team coach as it made a tour through the Wigan streets, first going through Pemberton where some of the players lived. It was a night to remember for a town that had already had many great Rugby League moments to savour.

And there was more to come . . .

11. A Royal occasion — Wigan players are presented to King George VI before the 1948 final.

12. Wembley action: Ken Gee and Cec Mountford swoop to halt a Bradford Northern break.

13-14. Moment of history. Joe Egan becomes the first player ever to receive the Challenge Cup from Royalty after the 1948 triumph over Bradford Northern. *below:* It's ours! Wigan skipper Joe Egan is carried triumphantly by his team-mates.

15. Another all-star Wigan line-up, this time from August 1949. *back row, left to right:* Nordgren, Hudson, McIntyre, Blan, Slevin, Gee. *centre:* Ratcliffe, Cunliffe, Ryan, Ashcroft, White. *front:* Bradshaw and Mountford.
16. Three Wigan greats from the teams of the Forties and Fifties — Cec Mountford, Martin Ryan and Tommy Bradshaw.

Wigan's Finest Hour

Whenever the great deeds of Wigan Rugby League Football Club are discussed the conversation inevitably turns to the year 1950 and one game in particular — the Championship final at Maine Road, Manchester, when 65,065 spectators were present at what many Wiganners still regard as the club's finest hour.

No fewer than eight of Wigan's star men were in the Great Britain tour party as the club prepared for the Championship final, taking on mighty Huddersfield. Martin Ryan, Jack Hilton, Gordon Ratcliffe, Tommy Bradshaw, Ken Gee, Joe Egan, Ernie Ashcroft and Jack Cunliffe were on their way to Australia with the Great Britain squad.

Wigan had enjoyed another great season, losing only four and drawing one of their thirty-six games to finish on top of the table. Huddersfield were second, six points behind, and Wigan had beaten Halifax after a replay in the semi-finals of the top four play-off.

Now, with so many international stars away, Wigan had to draw heavily on its reserves, but such was the wealth of talent within the club that it went on to score a memorable 20-2 victory with four tries and four goals, restricting mighty Huddersfield to a solitary goal. This is how the teams faced each other: Wigan fielded Ward, Silcock, Broome,

Roughley, Nordgren, Mountford, Alty, Slevin, McIntyre, Barton, Hudson, Large and Blan; Huddersfield fielded Hunter, Cracknell, Bawden, Devery, Cooper, Pepperell, Banks, Daly, Mumby, Wilmot, Morrison, Nicholson and Owens.

It was the perfect way to move into the Fifties — another great era in the history of the Wigan club. And just a year later that huge army of Wigan supporters was travelling south again to Wembley for the 1951 Challenge Cup final against Barrow.

The famous Wembley roar from 94,262 voices greeted the teams as they entered the arena. Wigan, captained by their New Zealand stand-off, Cec Mountford, lined up like this: Cunliffe, Hilton, Broome, Roughley, Nordgren, Mountford, Bradshaw, Gee, Curran, Barton, Silcock, Slevin and Blan.

Barrow's team was: Stretch, Lewthwaite, Jackson, Goodwin, Castle, Horne (capt), Toohey, Longman, McKinnell, Hartley, Grundy, Atkinson and McGregor.

Ken Gee gave Wigan early encouragement with a sixth minute penalty, but it was not until after almost an hour's play that the final produced its first try. Jack Hilton, later to become the Wigan club chairman, was again the opening

17. Wigan's Great Britain tourists from 1950. *back row, left to right:* Ratcliffe, Cunliffe, Egan, Hilton, Ashcroft. *front:* Ryan, Bradshaw, Gee.

try scorer, just as he had been at Wembley three years earlier. Then, late in the game mighty prop Ken Gee forced his way over and Mountford added the goal. There was extra joy for Mountford in receiving the trophy. He also became the first overseas player to win the Lance Todd Award as the outstanding player of the final.

Once again the town of Wigan was decked out in a sea of cherry and white when the Wigan players returned home with the Cup, but there was a slight hiccup to the proceedings at Wigan station when the first group of players went unrecognised by officials and were directed to an obscure rear entrance; but the slip was realised and the cup heroes were quickly re-routed to their official arrival point.

Wigan had a seven-year hitch to their Wembley ambitions in the Fifties and had to wait until 1958 for their next appearance in the Challenge Cup final, but they were always thereabouts and continued to be a dominant and highly entertaining force in the game.

While Wembley eluded them for a while, there was still the Championship, and in May 1952 Wigan supporters were heading across the Pennines for the Huddersfield Town FC ground and the Championship final against their great rivals Bradford Northern.

Northern had finished the table as leaders, and twice during the final they took the lead through the accurate goalkicking of fullback Joe Phillips. Wigan again showed their great trophy-winning qualities, however, with Jack Cunliffe snatching a brilliant try with a series of dummies at a crucial time to turn the game Wigan's way. Silcock and Ryan got Wigan's other tries and Ken Gee kicked two goals as the cherry and whites went on to win 13-6 in front of a crowd of 48,684. It was their eighth Championship Trophy triumph! The Championship contenders lined up like this: for Wigan there was Ryan, Hilton, Broome, Roughley,

Nordgren, Cunliffe, Alty, Gee, Mather, Woosey, Silcock, Large and Street; and for Bradford Northern, Phillips, Hawes, Mageen, Hastings, McLean, L Haley, Jones, Shreeve, N Haley, Radford, Tyler, Foster and Traill.

The Fifties continued to bring cup glory to Central Park, including two successive — and successful — Wembley trips in 1958 and 1959.

Wigan faced Workington Town in the 1958 final with the following team: Cunliffe, O'Grady, Ashton, Boston, Sullivan, Bolton, Thomas, Barton, Sayer, McTigue, Cherrington, Collier and McGurrin. Workington Town fielded McAvoy, Southward, O'Neil, Leatherbarrow, Wookey, Archer, Roper, Herbert, Eden, Key, Edgar, Thompson and Eve.

It was a thriller final with the Cumbrians taking Wigan all the way before the Lancashire club came through with a 13-9 victory with tries by Mick Sullivan, John Barton and Brian McTigue. Jack Cunliffe kicked two goals.

Eric Ashton, Wigan's captain, hoisted the trophy proudly aloft after his first Wembley final; the young centre was to make five more Wembley visits in an outstanding career as a player, as well as returning as a coach.

Coach Joe Egan and his players received a tumultuous reception as they toured Wigan in an open-topped coach, and the Mayor of Wigan, Councillor Oliver Bowers, spoke for everyone in the town when he thanked the players for "enhancing the name of Wigan".

Once again, Wigan were making a big contribution to Great Britain's tour of Australia and four of their stars — Eric Ashton, Dave Bolton, Mick Sullivan and Brian McTigue — missed the welcome home to link up with their tour colleagues.

20. Lancashire Cup Kings! Wigan skipper Cec Mountford hoists the County Trophy high after the victory against Warrington in the Lancashire Cup final of 1950. It came during a magnificent run of six successive years of triumph in the county competition from 1946.
21. Unbeatable! Wigan with their impressive array of trophies in this historic picture from 1950.

22. Winner! The try that opened the gates of Wembley. Brian Nordgren goes over to score for Wigan despite a last-gasp tackle by Brian Bevan — and Wigan have beaten Warrington in the 1951 semi-finals to reach Wembley!

23. Smiling all the way to Wembley! Wigan players in confident mood as they prepare to leave for the 1951 Cup final against Barrow.

24-25. Power play: mighty Wigan prop Ken Gee plunges through a couple of tackles to score in the 1951 final. *below:* We did it! Wigan captain Cec Mountford lifted shoulder-high with the Cup by his delighted team-mates after the win against Barrow.

26. Over the top . . . Wigan wing star Jack Hilton, who later became chairman of the club, finds his way barred by Harold Pimblett of Belle Vue Rangers during a game in January 1951 but puts in a clever kick over his opponent's head.

27. Season with a silver lining . . . Wigan players and officials proudly display trophies won in the 1951-52 campaign.
28. August 1955 and the start of a new season for Wigan. Ernie Ashcroft is the captain.

29. A picture which sums up the tremendous scoring power of Billy Boston, an all-time great Wigan hero. Boston shows why he was so unstoppable as a bunch of Hunslet defenders try to force him out at the corner flag during a match in 1958. The famous Welshman made a tremendous impact on the game after joining Wigan in 1953. He had played just five games for Wigan when he was chosen for the 1954 tour of Australia. He went on to have fifteen glorious seasons with the Central Park club, and scored a total of 571 tries — the most by any British player and surpassed only by Warrington Australian star Brian Bevan, the world record try-scorer. Twice Boston scored seven tries in a match. Boston also had an outstanding international record including 31 Test appearances for Great Britain. With centre Eric Ashton he formed one of the most famous wing partnerships in the history of Rugby League football.

"We'll Be Back"

Confident Wiganners were already predicting: "We'll be back at Wembley next year". And so they were, exactly thirty years since Wigan's first Wembley, and just twelve months later the mass exodus from Wigan took place again as the fans streamed south for the Challenge Cup final against Hull after an exciting 5-0 win over Leigh in the semi-finals.

They were hoping to see yet another piece of history from a team that had written itself into the Rugby League record books on so many previous occasions. This time the aim was Wembley victory in successive years — a feat no other side in the league had ever achieved.

The team had changed from the previous year. Fred Griffiths, a South African fullback and brilliant goalkicker, had joined the club. Keith Holden was in the centre and young loose forward Roy Evans, who had just missed out on the 1958 Wembley final because of illness, was there to take his Cup final place. Wigan fielded Griffiths, Boston, Ashton, Holden, Sullivan, Bolton, Thomas, Bretherton, Sayer, Barton, McTigue, Cherrington and Evans. Hull fielded Keegan, Cowan, Cooper, Saville, Watts, Mathews, Finn, Scott, Harris, J Drake, Sykes, W Drake and Whiteley.

Many of the pre-match predictions had said that the Hull pack would be the dominant force, but it was Wigan's day in no uncertain manner. They scorched home to a magnificent 30-13 victory with tries by Billy Boston (2), Keith Holden, Dave Bolton, Mick Sullivan and Brian McTigue. Fred Griffiths kicked six goals. Brian McTigue won the Lance Todd Trophy to add another honour to Wigan's memorable day.

Wigan wanted the hat trick of three successive Wembley finals, but it was not to be. Yorkshire took the honours in 1960 with Wakefield Trinity surpassing even Wigan's great win of the previous year. Hull again suffered the dejection of a Wembley dubbing, this time losing 38-5.

Wigan supporters never seem to have to wait long for a trophy, and May 1960 saw the Championship Cup back in the Central Park showcase after a decisive and impressive Wigan victory 27-3 against Wakefield Trinity in the finale at Odsal.

Wigan had finished thirteen points behind their great rivals St Helens in the final league table, but in the play-off for the title they disposed of the Saints in the semi-finals on their way to yet another chapter of glory for the club.

Once again Wigan packed a glittering array of talent into their line-up as they faced a Wakefield side also packed with outstanding players. They fielded Griffiths, Halliwell, Boston, Holden, Fenton, Ashton, Bolton, Barton, Sayer, Collier, McTigue, Lyon and Evans. Wakefield Trinity's players were Round, Smith, Skene, Fox, Etty, Rollin, Holliday, Wilkinson, Oakes, Vines, Firth, Chamberlain and Turner.

Eric Clay of Leeds was the referee and more than 83,000 people were in the vast Odsal bowl for this great finale to the season. Wigan, quite simply, took the match by storm with Billy Boston, who had been switched to centre, having a magnificent game. The power of the Wigan pack was another telling factor in a superb all-round performance by the Wigan team. Smith gave Trinity a flying start with a try after two minutes but after that it was one-way scoring with Eric Ashton and Billy Boston getting two tries and hooker Bill Sayer adding another while Fred Griffiths steered home six goals in a magnificent display of kicking.

30. The long walk. Wigan and Workington teams take the field for the 1958 Wembley final.

31-32. *above:* That's the style! Winger Mick Sullivan sprints over to score for Wigan in the 1958 Cup final. *below:* Cup triumph! Eric Ashton, the Wigan captain, is lifted high by his team-mates.

33. Heroes' welcome! The fans turn out in their thousands to greet Wigan players as they return home in triumph with the Challenge Cup in 1958.

34. *above :* Wembley action as scrum half Rees Thomas makes a break from a mid-field scrum during the 1959 Challenge Cup final against Hull. Wigan went on to win 30-13.
35. *right:* Wigan captain Eric Ashton is carried proudly by team-mates Norman Cherrington and John Barton after the runaway Wembley success against Hull.

36. Here we are again! The year is 1959 and it's another triumphant homecoming for Wigan's Wembley heroes.

37. The roar of the crowd — Wigan supporters pack the streets to welcome Wigan players on their arrival at the town hall with the Challenge Cup following the victory against Hull.

38. Mighty Brian McTigue as *Echo* Cartoonist Frank Barton saw him. McTigue gave outstanding service to Wigan and Great Britain, establishing himself as one of the finest forwards of all time. His ball-handling skills were legendary.

39. Early days for Billy Boston as he sprints down the wing during his first season with Wigan after coming north from the valleys of South Wales.

40. *below:* A try in the making. Billy Boston starts off on a 40-yard run which brought him a try in the match against Barrow at Central Park in August 1960.

41. Flashback to 1961 and an early-season picture of the Wigan line-up. *back row, left to right:* Bolton, Barton, McTigue, Boston, Evans, Collier, Entwistle. *front:* Griffiths, Sayer, Ashton, Bootle, Cherrington, Carlton.

42. More memories from the early Sixties. *back row, left to right:* Shillinglaw, Barton, Evans, Boston, C Clarke, J Clarke, A Stephens, Gilfedder, Sayer. *front:* Hill, Lako, Ashton, Parr, Ashby, Holden.

43. South African star Fred Griffiths, an outstanding fullback and goalkicker with Wigan in the Sixties.

Derby Final

Wigan had enjoyed two successful Wembley trips and a Championship triumph in successive seasons, and the cheers had hardly died away before they were back on the Wembley trail yet again. The year was 1961, and as round after round progressed it began to look more and more like a first ever derby final between those great rivals Wigan and St Helens.

The two sides have had some magnificent games over the years, packing Central Park and Knowsley Road in their traditional Easter and Christmas holiday fixtures. But the 'dream final' of a Wembley meeting had always eluded them.

Supporters in both towns held their breath as the draw for the Challenge Cup semi-finals was made. Then the cheers went up. Wigan and Saints had avoided each other again. The chance of that long-awaited Wembley derby was on!

First, however, the two rivals had to get over that last vital hurdle before the final. Hull were again moving strongly along the Wembley trail and faced St Helens in the semi-final at Odsal, but Saints made no mistake with a 26-9 victory, while Wigan were not to be denied another Wembley chance and accounted for Halifax 19-10 in their semi-final at Swinton.

So the great day dawned — and it was a sizzler! London basked in a heatwave, and as the temperature soared into the eighties the crowd of 94,672 basked in shirt sleeves and summer dresses. Many on the terraces fainted and had to be carried from the crowd.

It may have been hot on those terraces but it was a searing test for the players on the pitch. They rose to the task magnificently in what proved to be a thrilling final. Wigan lined up with Griffiths, Boston, Ashton (capt), Bootle, Carlton, Bolton, Entwistle, Barton, Sayer, McTigue, Lyon, Collier and Evans. Playing for St Helens were Rhodes, Vollenhoven, Large, McGinn, Sullivan, Murphy, Smith, Terry, Dagnail, Watson, Vines, Huddart and Karalius (capt).

Fullback Fred Griffiths gave Wigan an early lead with a penalty but some slick work by Vince Karalius and Dick Huddart sent Alex Murphy over for a try and just before half-time Austin Rhodes stretched the lead with a fine long-distance penalty goal.

Saints opened the second half well, but Griffiths pegged them back with another penalty, and when Billy Boston went charging down the wing in one of his typical blockbusting runs it took three defenders to save the day for Saints. It took one of the finest tries ever seen in a Rugby League Challenge Cup final at Wembley — and there have been many great scores over the years — to give St Helens a decisive edge and put Wigan's Cup hopes on the slide.

With little more than fifteen minutes to play Vollenhoven came racing away from deep inside the Saints' half. When he was headed off the South African wing star passed inside

44. Back on familiar ground. The club chairmen lead out their teams as Wigan *(right)* prepare to face St Helens in the first great derby final of 1961.

to his centre, Ken Large. The two thundered down-field and when Large was tackled he swung the ball out again to the wing where Vollenhoven rounded off a magnificent piece of attacking play by racing in for the try.

Rhodes added the goal kick and a penalty, but it was Saints' day with a 12-6 victory. To complete their afternoon Dick Huddart, that great Cumbrian forward, carried off the Lance Todd Trophy.

It was a disappointment for Wigan — but they proved their marvellous record of consistency and their ability to bounce back when in the following season (1961-62) they finished on top of the Rugby League table with the magnificent record of thirty-six games played, thirty-two won, only three defeats and one drawn game. In the top four play-off, however, they were beaten 13-11 by Huddersfield who went on to become Champions after finishing fourth in the table.

Wigan were back on the Wembley trail yet again in 1963, this time to take on the Cup holders, Wakefield Trinity, who had beaten Huddersfield the previous year.

Wigan had Dave Bolton playing at fullback with a three-quarter line-up of Billy Boston, Eric Ashton, Alan Davies and Frank Carlton; halfbacks were Stan McLeod and Frank Pitchford; and forwards were John Barton, Bill Sayer, Brian McTigue, Frank Collier, Geoff Lyon and Roy Evans.

It was a final when the need for substitutes in Rugby League football was emphasised in no uncertain manner as Wigan lost Bolton with concussion just before half-time and he was unable to return to the pitch until much later in the game. Wigan battled bravely, but Trinity went on to win 25-10. Wigan's points came from tries by Pitchford and Carlton with Ashton kicking two goals.

The Rugby League split into two divisions for the following two seasons — 1962-3 and 1963-4. Wigan finished eighth in the First Division for the first year of the move and were then runners-up to Swinton the following season.

Wembley Classic

In 1965 it was that old Wembley Magic again — and how! The Challenge Cup final between Wigan and Hunslet that year is still regarded as one of the all-time classic encounters in the history of Rugby League played at Wembley. It was a thriller from start to finish, full of great football skill and entertainment with some of the most spectacular scoring ever seen in a Challenge Cup final. Wigan pulled away to 20-9 at one stage but Hunslet came back in a breathtaking finish to close the final margin to 20-16. Wigan's points came with two tries by winger Trevor Lake and one each from Keith Holden and Laurie Gilfedder, who also kicked three goals. Eric Ashton got the other goal.

After such a closely contested final the voting for the Man of the Match was even closer — a dead heat in fact between Wigan fullback Ray Ashby, who had joined them from Liverpool City, and Hunslet winger Brian Gabbitas; they became the first players to share the Lance Todd Award.

This was Wigan's triumphant line-up: Ray Ashby, Billy Boston, Eric Ashton (capt), Keith Holden, Trevor Lake, Cliff Hill, Frank Parr, Danny Gardiner, Colin Clarke, Brian McTigue, Tony Stephens, Roy Evans and Laurie Gilfedder.

Wigan supporters were already regarding Wembley as their second home ground — and little wonder as the

45. Lord Derby shakes hands with Billy Boston as he is introduced to the Wigan players by skipper Eric Ashton before the 1961 Cup final.

Central Park side made yet another trip south to the final just twelve months after their victory against Hunslet.

Once again, it was their traditional rivals St Helens who provided Wigan with the chance to even the score for their defeat by the Saints five years earlier. But it was not to be. The record 98,536 crowd saw St Helens sweep to a 21-2 victory.

The magnificent long-range goalkicking of Lance Todd winner Len Killeen was one of the most telling factors of the final. He landed five goals in all and also scored a try, with others coming from John Mantle and Tommy Bishop and Alex Murphy adding a drop goal. Wigan's goal was kicked by Laurie Gilfedder.

Wigan's Wembley side was: Ray Ashby, Billy Boston, David Stephens, Eric Ashton (capt), Trevor Lake, Cliff Hill, Frank Parr, Danny Gardiner, Tom Woosey, Brian McTigue, Tony Stephens, Laurie Gilfedder and Harry Major.

It was to be another four years before Wigan returned to Wembley Stadium, but the 1968-69 season brought a new accolade for that lengthy Wigan scroll of honour. A new competition was providing Rugby League audiences with some exciting televised football on Tuesday nights in the early winter months, and Wigan were all set to make their mark once again.

The BBC2 Floodlit Trophy tournament had been launched in 1965 for clubs with floodlights, and eight teams took part in that first year. In 1968 Wigan carried off the trophy with an exciting 7-4 win against St Helens at Central Park watched by 13,479 spectators, one of the biggest final crowds in the history of the tournament.

Consistency has always been a key word in the achievements of the Wigan club, and that great quality was emphasised in the most impressive style when Wigan set up a winning sequence of league matches from the end of the 1968 season into the 1970-71 term which has never been beaten — no fewer than thirty-one successive victories!

Those famous twin towers of Wembley beckoned for the eleventh time for Wigan in 1970 — a record — and they travelled south to take on Castleford. Once more Wigan found themselves in the situation of taking on the holders of the trophy. Castleford had beaten Salford the previous May by 11-6.

Wigan fielded the following team for the 1970 final: Colin Tyrer, Keri Jones, Bill Francis, Peter Rowe, Kevin O'Loughlin, David Hill, Frank Parr, Keith Ashcroft, Bob Burdell, Brian Hogan, Bill Ashurst, David Robinson and a new captain, Doug Laughton, at loose forward. It was the first Wembley final to have substitutes: Wigan had Cliff Hill and Colin Clarke on the bench, and Hill was soon to join the fray as Colin Tyrer, a talented fullback with a magnificent goalkicking record who had joined Wigan from Leigh, had to go off with a bad facial injury only sixteen minutes into the game.

Castleford led 5-2 at half-time with a try by Alan Lowndes and a goal from Mick Redfearn in reply to an early Tyrer goal for Wigan.

The cherry and whites battled hard to try to pull the match back in the second half, but Castleford kept their noses in front with Redfearn landing a further penalty to make the final margin of this closely fought final 7-2.

Disappointment in finals seemed to shadow Wigan: when they won their way through to the Championship play-off final twelve months later they went down again, this time to rivals St Helens with a 16-12 defeat at Station

46. So near . . . winger Frank Carlton races over for Wigan in the 1961 final but the whistle has gone for a forward pass and it is no

Road, Swinton.

But it had been a magnificent league season by the Central Park club in which they had lost only four of their thirty-four matches and finished at the top of the table to take the League Leaders' Trophy, just two points ahead of Saints.

David Robinson and Bill Ashurst scored tries with Ashurst also landing two goals and Colin Tyrer kicking a goal. But it was not enough as Saints scored tries through Billy Benyon and Bob Blackwood and skipper Kel Coslett landed five goals to take the trophy.

Nevertheless, hardly a year went by without Wigan making their mark in one competition or another and they were soon reasserting their authority in the Lancashire Cup competition in the early Seventies. They faced their great rivals Widnes in the 1971 final for the first time since the 1945-46 thriller when Widnes had pipped them at the post for the trophy.

Both teams were packed with top talent as they lined up for the final at Knowsley Road in front of a disappointingly low attendance of just 6,970. Wigan's team was Tyrer, Eastham, Francis, Fuller, Wright, D Hill, Ayres, Ashcroft, Clarke, Fletcher, Ashurst, K O'Loughlin and D Laughton, who later went on to coach Widnes to some of their most memorable trophy triumphs. Widnes lined up: Dutton, Brown, McLoughlin, Aspey, Gaydon, O'Neill, Bowden, Warlow, Foran, Doughty, Kirwan, Walsh and Nicholls.

Wigan went on to win the Cup with a fine 15-8 victory in which Eastham, Francis and Ayres scored tries and Tyrer kicked three goals.

Two years later Wigan were back in the Lancashire Cup final, this time taking on Salford at Wilderspool Stadium.

Wigan's team had shown quite a few changes during the two seasons since their last Lancashire Cup final appearance. They faced Salford with this line-up: Francis, Vigo, D Hill, Kieron O'Loughlin, Wright, Cassidy, Ayres, Smethurst, Clarke, Gray, Irving, D Robinson and Cunningham. Salford fielded Charlton, Fielding, Watkins, Hesketh, Holland, Gill, Banner, Mackay, Walker, Davies, Dixon, Kear and Prescott.

Rugby at that time was not enjoying the best of support, and compared with more recent seasons the attendance of just 8,012 was disappointing. But for the Wiganners in that Wilderspool crowd it was another day of celebration as their team ran home winners by 19-9. O'Loughlin scored two tries and Wright one try; Gray kicked four goals and Ayres landed one. But as the jubilant Wigan supporters streamed out of Wilderspool Stadium that winter afternoon in 1973 they could have been excused for looking at you in disbelief if you had told them that it was the last time in the Seventies that a major trophy would be seen at Central Park. They did, however, win their way through to the Lancashire Cup final again in the 1977-78 season, only to suffer defeat at the hands of Workington Town.

The Cumbrians won 16-13 in the final at Warrington for their one and only trophy success in this competition to date. Wigan put up a formidable show with tries from Willicombe, Nulty and Ashurst, plus a goal each from Nulty and Burke, but it was not enough to prevent the trophy from going back to Cumbria.

The Rugby League made the momentous decision to split into two-division football in the Seventies for the first

47a. The year is 1963. Wigan are back at Wembley. Their opponents are Wakefield Trinity and in this piece of action Wigan centre Alan Davies halts a break by Trinity stand-off Harold Poynter.

time since the 1963-64 season. The great divide came at the start of the 1973-74 campaign and Wigan struggled to make an impression in the league, finishing sixth from the bottom of the sixteen-club table in their first season in Division One. But the next year saw them finishing runners-up to St Helens.

In terms of trophies won, however, the Seventies were not as productive for Wigan as other years, and when season 1979-80 came to a close the Central Park club found themselves in the almost unbelievable situation of suffering relegation into Second Division football. Wigan finished fourth from the bottom and went down along with Hunslet, York and Blackpool Borough. They had won only nine of their thirty games and drawn three. Points scored against them totalled 523.

But you can't keep Wigan down for long! They have always shown that great quality for bouncing back against the odds, and they stormed straight back into First Division football after one season in the lower section where they won twenty and drew three of their twenty-eight matches to finish just three points behind Second Division Champions York.

At that stage, no doubt, many Wigan fans would just have settled for a period of consolidation in the league, making sure that Wigan never again tasted relegation.

47b. Echo cartoonist's impression of 1965 Lance Todd winner Ray Ashby

48. One of the greatest moments of any player's career — that walk out of the famous Wembley tunnel on Cup final day. This was Wigan's entrance into the great arena alongside Hunslet for the 1965 final which proved to be one of the most memorable finals of all time.

49-50. Ray Ashby sweeps up from fullback to make a dynamic break for Wigan during the win against Hunslet. Ashby, who had joined Wigan from Liverpool City, went on to share the Lance Todd Award with Hunslet's Brian Gabbitas. *below:* The smiles say it all! A hug from Eric Ashton and a pat on the back from Billy Boston for centre Keith Holden after he has scored against Hunslet.

51. The moment they have waited for — Eric Ashton receives the Challenge Cup from Princess Alexandra following the victory over Hunslet.

52. *below:* Wigan halfbacks Cliff Hill and Frank Parr lead their team-mates with the Trophy in the 1965 Wembley lap of honour.

53. *above right:* Famous double act — Eric Ashton and the Rugby League Challenge Cup! The brilliant Wigan captain proudly holds the Trophy after the 1965 triumph.

54. Wembley hat trick! Roy Evans and Laurie Gilfedder wearing supporters' hats, 1965 style.

55. The date is 21 May 1966. Prime Minister Harold Wilson is introduced to the Wigan players before the Wembley final against St Helens.

56. Wembley handshake — Wigan skipper Eric Ashton and Saints captain Alex Murphy, watched by referee Harry Hunt, greet each other before the 1966 Challenge Cup final.

57. Derby action during the Wigan v Saints clash at Wembley and Trevor Lake and Cliff Hill put the brakes on a dash by Tom van Vollenhoven.

58. The Wembley scene switches to 1970 as Wigan return yet again to the Challenge Cup final. Their skipper Doug Laughton leads out the players for the match against Castleford.

59. Wigan prop Keith Ashcroft goes straight between the posts during the 1970 final but it's disappointment for Wigan because there has been a forward pass and a try is ruled out.

60. Fullback Colin Tyrer is carried off injured during the 1970 Cup final.

61. No way through! Redfearn of Castleford finds his way barred by Doug Laughton, Bob Burdell and David Robinson.

62. The year is 1971 and the Lancashire Cup is back at Central Park. Wigan captain Doug Laughton is swamped by young fans after the victory at Knowsley Road against Widnes.

Glorious Eighties

Wigan did consolidate — and a whole lot more! The Glorious Eighties were about to dawn for the Central Park club!

The loyal Wigan supporters who stood their ground on the terraces through a season of Second Division football in 1980-81 were about to see that loyalty and confidence in their club rewarded, and rewarded in the most spectacular way imaginable as Wigan boldly carved out one of the most successful chapters ever seen in the club's history.

Wigan had sampled the glory years in the past, but even some of those great deeds were overshadowed by the achievements of the Eighties. Back to Wembley they went in 1984, 1985, 1988 and 1989 with the Challenge Cup being carried home in pride once more from the 1985, 1988 and 1989 finals. And there was more . . . much more.

In April 1987, for the first time since Eric Ashton and his men had won the Rugby League Championship twenty-seven years earlier, the League Championship flag fluttered proudly over Central Park. Wigan did it in such style! Their team of all stars romped away to the Championship. They had it all wrapped up more than a fortnight before the end of the league programme and finished no fewer than fifteen points ahead of their nearest rivals St Helens in a record-breaking season.

It was the season when Wigan fans reckoned you could see a silver glow over Central Park — emanating from the trophy showcase! And no wonder as Wigan rounded off a truly memorable campaign by also capturing the Lancashire Cup, the John Player Trophy and the Premiership Trophy!

In fact, every major award has come to Central Park during the memorable Eighties, including a new honour which once again saw Wigan as world leaders — in every sense — as they staged one of the most memorable nights of Rugby League World Club Champions by beating Australian Kingpins Manly.

The John Player competition provided the first trophy success of the Eighties when Wigan defeated Leeds in the 1982-83 final at Elland Road, Leeds — the first time the Leeds United soccer ground had been the setting for the final of this competition. A crowd of 19,553 saw Wigan win 15-4 after being down 4-3 at half-time. Their two tries both came from the left wing with Henderson Gill scoring the first. He had to go off injured later on in the game and his substitute, Brian Jullif, scored the other try shortly before the end. Colin Whitfield kicked three goals and also landed a drop goal. Martin Foy, the Wigan stand off, earned the Man of the Match award.

Wigan's growing army of support travelled home joyfully over the Pennines and before long they were making plans for an even longer journey — back to Wembley and another Challenge Cup final for the first time in fourteen years. And it was Derby Day with those traditional rivals Widnes as the opposition for the 1984 final.

Wigan hit the headlines by flying Balmain prop Kerry Hemsley in from Australia to play in the final. They fielded Edwards, Ramsdale, Stephenson, Whitfield, Gill, Cannon,

63. More Lancashire Cup action, this time from the 1985 final, and it's a spectacular piece of scoring for Ellery Hanley as he goes through the air to touch down against Warrington.

Stephens, Hemsley, H Tamati, Case, West (capt), Scott and Pendlebury. Widnes lined up like this: Burke, Wright, Hughes, Lydon, Basnett, O'Loughlin, Gregory, S O'Neill, Elwell, K Tamati, Gorley, M O'Neill and Adams (capt).

It was a particularly memorable day for Shaun Edwards, the Wigan fullback, who was the youngest player ever to appear in a Wembley final up to that date. Shaun was just 17 years, 6 months and 19 days old when he walked confidently out of that vast Wembley tunnel with his Wigan team-mates for the greatest occasion in any player's career.

Wigan hopes ran high, but by one of those ironic twists of football fate it was a lad who had been born in Wigan and actually played for their under-11s schoolboy side there nine years earlier who put the skids under the Central Park club's Cup dream.

Joe Lydon, later to join Wigan in a record transfer deal from Widnes, stole the show with two spectacular long-distance tries in a performance which earned him the Lance Todd Trophy. The rest of the Widnes points came from a try by Kieron O'Loughlin, three goals by Mick Burke and a drop goal from Steve O'Neill, a former Wigan player. Hemsley got Wigan's try and Colin Whitfield kicked a goal. Widnes won 19-6.

As I left Wembley that afternoon I heard one Cockney souvenir-seller tell a dejected young Wigan supporter: "Don't worry son, you'll be back next year."

The words were prophetic! Just twelve months later Wigan's massive cherry and white army was moving south to take Wembley by storm once again. This time it was a Battle of the Roses and Hull were the opposition in a match which packed Wembley Stadium. And what a match it turned out to be for that capacity crowd of 97,801.

Wigan and Hull produced one of the most spectacular games ever seen at Wembley. It was the kind of match when if you blinked you missed some exciting action. It was packed with spectacular attacking football, tremendous defence and outstanding try-scoring with a breathtaking finish as Hull pulled back to close the gap to 28-24 at the end.

One of the most fascinating duels was at halfback between two great Australian Test players, Wigan's Brett Kenny and Hull's Peter Sterling, with Kenny narrowly beating his Aussie Test team-mate for the Lance Todd Trophy as Man of the Match.

Wigan carried off their win with two tries from Ferguson and one each by Edwards, Gill and Kenny. Gill kicked three goals and Stephenson landed one. Hull replied with two tries from Leuluai, one each by James, Evans and Divorty who came on as a substitute for Puckering, and two goals from Crooks.

It had been the highest scoring final since the competition began and the teams who provided that thriller lined up like this: for Wigan, Edwards, Ferguson, Stephenson, Donlan, Gill, Kenny, M Ford, Courtney, Kiss, Case, West, Dunn and Potter; and for Hull, Kemble, James, Evans, Leuluai, O'Hara, Ah Kuoi, Sterling, Crooks, Patrick, Puckering, Muggleton, Rose and Norton.

It was a wet weekend in Wigan when the team brought home the Cup but the weather could not dampen the spirits of the thousands who turned out to greet their team. Skipper Graeme West held the Cup high and told the crowds: "You are the greatest supporters in the land!" And those fans certainly knew how to support their side! Wigan attendances in the Eighties soared and soared with Rugby League interest booming in the town. And they had plenty to cheer about!

The echoes of Wembley had hardly faded away before

64. Australian halfback Steve Ella reaches out to touch down for one of his two tries against Warrington in the Lancashire Cup final of 1985.

Wigan were setting the pulses racing again. They opened the 1985-86 season in spectacular style, giving their loyal army of supporters yet another trophy — this time one that was new to Central Park. The old saying "Show Wigan a cup and it's theirs" which had originated in the Fifties must have been on the minds of their long-serving fans when Wigan came home from a pre-season visit to the Isle of Man with another 'first'.

The Rugby League had introduced the idea of a pre-season Charity Shield match on the Manx Island between Cup winners and Champions. Wigan went there to face Hull Kingston Rovers and immediately stamped their mark on the competition by sweeping to a magnificent 34-6 victory with two tries each from Steve Donlan and Henderson Gill, one try from Mike Ford and seven goals from the boot of David Stephenson. In addition, Shaun Edwards, playing at stand-off, earned the Man of the Match award.

Next, the Lancashire Cup, which was virtually a piece of private property at Central Park over the years — Wigan hold the record for most final appearances and most wins in the competition — was once more destined for its familiar resting place in Wigan colours.

And they did it in style with a 34-8 victory against Warrington at St Helens to set yet another record for the competition with the highest final score.

Another Australian, halfback Steve Ella, carried off the Man of the Match award this time, having scored two of the Wigan tries. Others came from Shaun Edwards, Ellery Hanley and Nicky Kiss. David Stephenson steered home seven goals.

The winning line-up was: Edwards, Henley-Smith, Stephenson, Hanley, Whitfield, Ella, M Ford, Dowling, Kiss, Wayne, Du Toit, Goodway and Potter.

Yet another trophy was to follow in the same season as Wigan swept to victory in the John Player Special Trophy competition by defeating Hull Kingston Rovers 11-8 in the final at Elland Road, watched by a crowd of 17,573. Mike Ford and Shaun Wayne got the tries with David Stephenson kicking one goal and Greg Dowling, the Australian prop forward, adding a drop goal.

The cheers of the Wigan fans echoed around the Leeds United ground as the players paraded the trophy. The victorious line-up was Hampson, Mortd, Stephenson, Hanley, Gill, Ella, M Ford, Dowling, Kiss, Wayne, West, Goodway and Potter.

Wigan also gave everyone a thrilling run for their money in the Championship stakes when they finished as runners-up to Halifax who just pipped them at the post with forty-four points to Wigan's forty-three. Wigan nevertheless finished with the best scoring record in the First Division, piling up 776 points in their thirty games and conceding only 300.

So near, yet so far. Throughout all their years of achievement in the various cup competitions, the one trophy which had eluded Wigan longer than any other was the Championship. But the 1986-87 season would put that right and take the first league title to Central Park for twenty-seven years.

And not only that! Wigan gave an early indication that it was going to be a season of extra special vintage when they raced through to the Lancashire Cup final, running up fifty-two points against Rochdale Hornets in the first round, walloping Whitehaven for seventy-four in round two and then beating the 'old enemy' St Helens 22-16 in the semi-finals.

Oldham provided the opposition for the final at St

65. Heads we win! Hooker Nicky Kiss tries a new line in headgear as he takes the Trophy around the pitch with team-mates Andy Goodway and Nicky du Toit after the Lancashire Cup success against Warrington in 1985.

Helens where a crowd of 20,180 turned out — only the second time in twenty-two years that a Lancashire Cup final had topped the 20,000 mark.

Wigan won handsomely by 27-6 with two tries from Shaun Edwards and others by Mike Ford and Joe Lydon, who also landed a drop goal. Henderson Gill kicked five goals.

This was the victorious team: Edwards, Lydon, Stephenson, Bell, Gill, Hanley, Ford, West, Dermott, Case, Roberts, Potter and Goodway. It was a marvellous start for their new coach, Graham Lowe, the New Zealand international coach who had been brought over to Central Park.

The Lancashire Cup was only the start of a season which would go into the Wigan record books as one of the most memorable of all time. Wigan were also going strongly in the league. They had reeled off wins in their first five games before going down at Warrington on 5 October. But it was only a temporary set-back. The wins, the points and the big crowds continued to pile up in impressive numbers at Central Park.

Their next trophy objective in that memorable 1986-87 campaign was the John Player competition. Lowe's men overcame Leeds, Swinton, Leigh and Hull on their way to the final. Their opponents were Warrington who had beaten them at Central Park on New Year's Day and proved to be the only side to defeat Wigan in the entire season in league football.

Warrington were favourites. They had overwhelmed Widnes in the semi-finals and had a victory sequence stretching over fourteen consecutive games behind them when they lined up against Wigan in the final at Burden Park, Bolton (the first time a major Rugby League occasion had been staged at the Bolton Wanderers' FC ground).

A crowd of 21,144 turned out, paying £86,041 in receipts, and the fans in the cherry and white saw their team carry off a momentous victory.

Wigan won 18-4 and, as on so many occasions in the past, they made it another great 'first' for Central Park by becoming the first club to retain the John Player Special Trophy. It also equalled Warrington's great record of three trophy final wins — and provided the widest winning margin for the final of the competition.

Henderson Gill scored two of the tries and also kicked a goal, while other tries came from Andy Goodway and Dean Bell. This was the triumphant line-up: Hampson, Stephenson, Lydon, Bell, Gill, Hanley, Edwards, West, Dermott, Case, Roberts, Potter and Goodway. With two trophies tucked away, the big question on the Central Park terraces was whether Wigan could make it a clean sweep of trophies.

It must have been uppermost in the minds of the vast army of Central Park supporters as the Silk Cut Challenge Cup and the hope of another Wembley visit loomed on the horizon. Wigan had continued to make outstanding progress in the league and they sailed through their preliminary round Challenge Cup match against Workington with a 68-0 romp. But round one brought a jolt. Wigan struggled at Watersheddings as the home side pulled off a shock 10-8 win after Wigan had led 8-4 with just a couple of minutes to go. The Wembley dream had been shattered — but the Championship and Premiership lived on. And how!

Wigan continued to dominate the First Division and

from that New Year's Day defeat against Warrington they never lost another league match. Central Park supporters not only enjoyed a great winning run but also highly entertaining and high-scoring football. Bradford Northern were hammered 60-6 and Leeds 30-0 — at Headingley, too! Wakefield Trinity felt the might of Wigan's scoring power as they went down 72-6 on their own ground. Featherstone Rovers had sixty-two points scored against them and then it was sweet revenge against Oldham as Wigan ran up fifty-four points and kept their own line firmly intact. Even St Helens in the traditional Easter fixture could not put the brakes on Wigan's relentless drive towards the Championship. Saints were beaten 42-12 at Central Park.

The latter results of the league programme, though, were merely a formality. When Wigan hammered Featherstone Rovers on 5 April they made sure of the title with two weeks of the First Division fixture list still to run! And they did it in such style! Not only did they finish fifteen points ahead of their nearest challengers, St Helens, but they also set a new series of records for First Division football — records which had all previously been held by their traditional Knowsley Road rivals.

Wigan finished with the most points — 941 — topping the previous best of 920 by St Helens. They earned the best haul of league points with fifty-six from twenty-eight wins and they set new records for the least number of tries conceded (twenty-nine in the entire league season) and the least points (just 193 were scored against that solid Wigan defence). At the same time Wigan set a new record for the most tries in a First Division campaign with their total of 174.

What a Championship campaign! And there was an extra individual record to grace the achievement with Ellery Hanley, another great name for the Wigan Hall of Fame who had been signed by Wigan in a record £150,000 transfer in 1985, notching up a Division One record haul of forty-four tries, including five tries in one game which equalled the existing record.

Wigan were the talk of the Rugby League — and no wonder. Yet there was still another major honour to be won in that tremendous 1986-87 campaign.

The Premiership Trophy would add the crowning touch to Wigan's great season. And so it proved to be as Graham Lowe's men proved unstoppable once again. They accounted for Widnes by 22-18 in a Central Park thriller after being 14-6 down at one stage. Then they knocked out that season's Wembley winners Halifax 18-10 in the semi-finals in front of a crowd of 22,443 after coming from behind.

The final brought a derby clash with their great rivals Warrington at Old Trafford in the first Premiership double-decker event ever staged. It was a wet, miserable and cold afternoon but the weather did not keep away the crowds. They turned out in force to produce a Premiership final record of 38,756.

Wigan provided the perfect finishing touch to a magnificent season for their supporters by pulling off an 8-0 win with a try by Joe Lydon and goals from Henderson Gill and David Stephenson.

This is how their team took the field: Hampson, Gill, Stephenson, Bell, Lydon, Edwards, Gregory, Case, Kiss, Wane, Goodway, Potter and Hanley.

Wigan supporters went on holiday that summer still talking about the magnificent achievements of the past season — and eagerly looked forward to the start of the new campaign. Would 1987-88 bring more trophy success to Central Park? The answer was not long in coming!

Wigan travelled to the Isle of Man for the Okells Charity Shield match — Champions against Cup winners — on 23 August and started where they had left off the previous May with yet another success.

Graham Lowe's men took on Halifax, who had won the trophy the previous season, and beat them convincingly. Wigan scored forty-four points with only twelve conceded, thanks to tries by Edwards (2), Bell (2), Hampson (2) and Gill and eight goals from Stephenson. This was their line-up: Hampson, Stephenson, Byrne, Bell, Gill, Edwards, Gregory, West, Kiss, Case, Gildart, Potter and Goodway.

It was the perfect way to start a season, and within weeks Wigan were to achieve one of the greatest honours — if not *the* greatest honour — in the club's history.

Tremendous work had been put in to stage a World Club Championship between Wigan and the Australian Sydney Premiership winners, Manly-Warringah.

On 7 October 1988 the dream became a spectacular reality as Wigan lined up against the Australian kingpins in front of a magnificent Central Park crowd of 36,895. True to Wigan enterprise and style, the big game had all the razzmatazz and presentation you would expect for such an important world event — and more. Wigan set the scene perfectly. The atmosphere inside Central Park was electric — and the two teams responded with an epic game to meet the occasion. This is how they faced each other: Wigan fielded Hampson, Russell, Stephenson, Lydon, Gill, Edwards, Gregory, Case, Kiss, Wane, Goodway, Potter and Hanley. Manly fielded Shearer, Ronson, Williams, O'Connor, Davis, Lyons, Hasler, Daley, Cochrane, Gatley, Gibbs, Cunningham and Vautin.

Wigan carried off the world crown with a thrilling 8-2 win with four penalty goals by David Stephenson in reply to a goal by Michael O'Connor for Manly, who had forward Ron Gibbs dismissed in the forty-fifth minute.

The tremendous tackling by both sides was a big feature of a pulsating game which might not have had any tries but was nevertheless brimming over with excitement. And apart from earning their title as the world's greatest, Wigan also provided a massive boost for British Rugby League in general.

The cheers had hardly faded away from this momentous occasion before Wigan were moving straight into their preparation for yet another major final. Just four days after beating Manly, Wigan, with an unchanged side, took on

66. A night to remember! Wigan in action against Australian kingpins Manly in the World Club Championship challenge match at Central Park in October 1987. This was one of the most memorable occasions in the history of the Wigan club as the cherry and whites brought off a magnificent victory in a pulsating game. Here Ian Potter tries to break from the tackle of Paul Vautin to set up

Warrington in the final of the Grunhalle Lancashire Cup at Knowsley Road and carried off the trophy for the third successive season. Wigan's 28-16 victory came with tries from Hanley (2), Gill and West, who had come on as substitute for Wane. Lydon kicked five goals and Stephenson added one.

Only one winner's medal remained outstanding from the remarkable collection that Wigan coach Graham Lowe had amassed during his short time at the club. He was only in his second season but had already steered the side to Championship, Premiership, John Player Special Trophy, the Lancashire Cup (twice) and the Charity Shield successes. Now only Wembley remained to complete a spectacular two-season period of every honour in the game for the Wigan boss. Could Wigan do it? Could they make Wembley and win the Silk Cut Challenge Cup for a record eighth time at the famous stadium?

The draw for the first round put luck on Wigan's side with a home tie against Bradford Northern. But that was where the luck ended because Northern were a tough obstacle to overcome and they ran Wigan desperately close in a titanic Central Park struggle where Joe Lydon's thirty-fifth minute penalty goal provided the only points of the match.

Round Two brought Yorkshire opposition once again — and another home tie. Leeds raced off to a great start with ten quick points on the board but Wigan showed their great powers of recovery to come back and win 30-14.

The home ties held good when the third round pairings were made and Wigan faced Widnes — Wigan won by 10-1. The semi-finals brought Wigan into opposition with Salford in testing, muddy conditions at Burnden Park, Bolton, but Wigan won the day in style with a 34-4 victory to book that Wembley prize.

Wigan must have looked like a ghost town on the afternoon of 30 April. Just about everyone who could get to the final was inside Wembley, part of a capacity 94,273 crowd, paying world record receipts of £1,102,247. The rest were glued to their television and radio sets as the whole town willed the Central Park club to win and provide their

67. Up and under! This Manly player is firmly held by three Wigan tacklers.

coach Graham Lowe with one remaining winner's medal to make the glittering full set.

At the same time the blue and white colours of Halifax also filled a massive swathe of the Wembley terraces as they, too, hoped it would be an extra special occasion for their coach, Australian Chris Anderson, in his farewell after a magnificent period with the club which had included a Wembley victory over St Helens twelve months earlier.

Wigan's team lined up like this: Lydon, Tony Iro, Kevin Iro, Bell, Gill, Edwards, Gregory, Case, Kiss, Shelford, Goodway, Potter and Hanley. Halifax fielded Eadie, Meredith, Tony Anderson, Wilkinson, Whitefield, Grogan, Robinson, James, McCallion, Neller, Holliday, Dixon and Pendlebury.

Wigan ran away with the match giving a magnificent seven-try display. They had the final all wrapped up long before the end and were leading 26-0 within a few minutes of the start of the second half as they revelled in Wembley's wide acres to turn on a sparkling display of attacking football. But Halifax, to their everlasting credit, stuck to their task in magnificent style to pull back two tries in the second half, and they also produced some fine footballing spells. On the day, though, they were clearly second best to an outstanding Wigan outfit and also had their plans disrupted when loose forward Les Holliday had to go off with a knee injury after just twenty minutes.

Wigan were magnificent. Their tries came from Kevin Iro (2), Tony Iro, Lydon, Hanley, Bell and Gill with Gregory and Lydon each kicking a goal to reach a final score of 32-12.

Andy Gregory's superb display at scrum half, the springboard for so many of Wigan's great attacking efforts, earned him the Lance Todd Award as the outstanding player of the final.

Afterwards in the dressing room coach Graham Lowe summed up everyone's thoughts when he told his players: "You were magnificent. No one could have lived with you out there today."

68. The brilliant handling skills of halfback Andy Gregory set up a Wigan move as he tries to prise open the Manly cover.

69-70. More action from the Big One — the World Challenge match — with Manly halfback Des Hasler trying to find a way through Wigan's defence. *below:* Down he goes! Wigan prop forward Brian Case plunges a Manly player to the ground to halt another Australian raid in the World Challenge game.

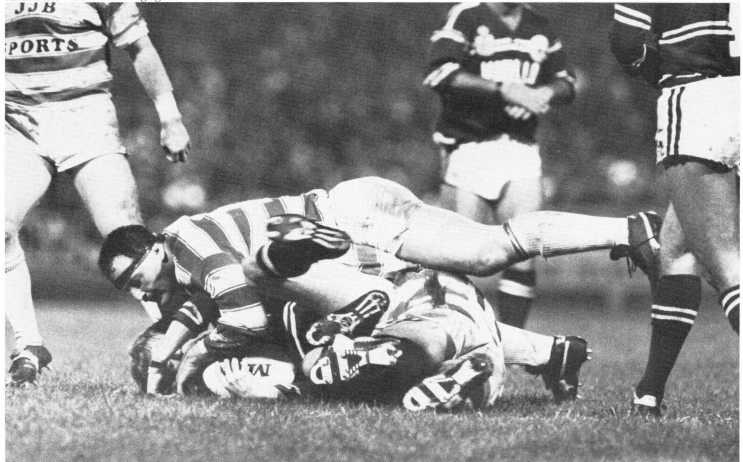

71. The scorching pace of Shaun Edwards as he races through the Manly defence during the big Central Park challenge match, watched by a magnificent crowd of 36,895.

72. A fine action shot of powerful New Zealand threequarter Kevin Iro, one of the many overseas stars who have come to Central Park over the years and made a big impact on the British game.

73. Wigan have had some great wing stars over the years — including one of their current Great Britain internationals, Henderson Gill.

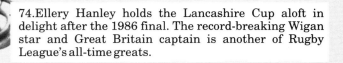

74.Ellery Hanley holds the Lancashire Cup aloft in delight after the 1986 final. The record-breaking Wigan star and Great Britain captain is another of Rugby League's all-time greats.

75. The way to Wembley — Shaun Edwards makes a fine break during the Challenge Cup semi-final against Salford at Bolton in 1988. Wigan opened the gates to Wembley in marvellous style with an emphatic 34-4 win.

76. Wembley 1988 — a perfect setting for the fluent football skills of any side and Wigan displayed theirs to the full in a magnificent performance of Rugby League football at its best to beat Halifax 32-12. Two of those tries came from New Zealand star Kevin Iro. This is his first — a great effort on a day of great scoring.

77. The famous Trophy, which has been carried home in pride so many times by so many Wigan teams of the past, wears the famous cherry and white colours yet again as the heroes of 1988 celebrate their momentous victory.

78. Back home to a tremendous welcome from the loyal Rugby League public of Wigan — and a greeting from the players for their supporters. Hooker Nicky Kiss takes the microphone to greet the crowd while club chairman Mauric Lindsey (*left*) and the players share the enjoyment.

79. The man behind the team — Wigan' brilliant coach, Graham Lowe, who steered the side to success in every Rugby League competition within two years of arriving a Central Park.

80. *top:* The Lancashire Cup is on its way 'back home' to Central Park as Wigan players line up with the Trophy after yet another success in the competition — this time 1988.

81. *left:* Wigan have also made a big impact on the John Player Special Trophy competition. Ellery Hanley, the Wigan captain, proudly displays the Trophy after the club's 1989 success.

82. *above:* Stepping out . . . Wigan fullback Steve Hampson in a typical attacking sortie.

83. Captain's style . . . Wigan skipper Ellery Hanley makes a dash for the line.
84. A try all the way . . . Joe Lydon shows his exciting pace in a brilliant touch-line dash.

85. Quick tackling . . . prop forward Ian Lucas gets to grips with Saints' stand-off Shane Cooper as he attempts to break through.

86. Driving force . . . Wigan's New Zealand threequarter Tony Iro in a determined attacking burst.

87. Centre power . . . Kevin Iro sweeps forward with brother Tony in support.

88. Crunch! . . . Adrian Shelford is the man with the ball in this three-man tackle.

95. More action from the Maine Road thriller in which Wigan clinch their 1989 Wembley final.
96. *below:* Hard going for Hanley. Wigan skipper Ellery is well surrounded by Warrington defenders during the Maine Road semi-final.
97.*opposite page:* Another of Wigan's many international stars — Shaun Edwards.

98. Tony Iro in action at Maine Road.
99. Andy Platt tests the defence.

100. The mighty boot of Joe Lydon proved crucial in the Maine Road victory against Warrington with a sensational drop goal from inside his own half.

101. Wigan prop forward Ian Lucas.
102. *below:* More action from the semi-final victory against Warrington at the Manchester City ground.

103. Graham Lowe and his men step out of the big Wembley tunnel and into the arena for the 1989 Silk Cut Challenge Cup final.
104. Wembley action . . . Steve Hampson shapes up to halt a run by Paul Groves. Shaun Edwards is also moving up with a challenge.

105. Wembley action . . . Les Quirk makes a break for Saints but Ian Potter, Ellery Hanley and Nicky Kiss are challenging.
106. Wembley action . . . try-scorer Kevin Iro walks back from the line after touching down for Wigan.

107. Wembley action . . . Andy Gregory kicks through in fine style.

108. Wembley action . . . Saints prop Tony Burke finds himself outnumbered.

109. Wembley action . . . a picture to capture that magical atmosphere of the final.
110. *below:* Wembley action . . . Wigan attack comes to a halt.
111. *opposite page:* Wembley action . . . up and under! Steve Hampson, Ellery Hanley and Saints fullback
Garry Connolly go up for the ball.

112. Wembley action ... hard going for Roy Haggerty as Andy Platt and Nicky Kiss move in to make the tackle.
113. Victory in sight ... Wigan coach Graham Lowe with forwards Ian Potter and Nicky Kiss alongside him on the Wembley bench.
It is late in the game and there can be no doubt about the result as Wigan surge on to their great trophy triumph.

114. Magical moment as Wigan players show the Trophy to their delighted supporters.
115. Lap of honour and supporters show their joy as Ellery holds the Trophy.

116. Wembley wonders! Graham Lowe and his men line up for the photographers after completing a magnificent victory.

1988-89 Season

Wigan were soon hot on the trail of major honours again in the new season. They suffered disappointment in the pre-season Okells Charity Shield match in the Isle of Man where their close rivals Widnes scored a 20-14 victory before a crowd of just over 5,000, but it was only a temporary check to Wigan's drive to bring more silverware back to Central Park.

Within three weeks of the start of the season the Wigan fans were already cheering their team home to a cup tie success which proved to be the launching pad for yet another competition triumph.

In the first round of the Grunhalle Lancashire Cup Wigan pulled out a visit to Barrow. They took it in their stride with a 24-10 win to line up a second round home tie against Rochdale Hornets. A crowd of more than 7,700 turned up at Central Park to see Wigan romp home 36-4. But if that had been a comparatively easy hurdle, the semi-

final stage brought one of the toughest challenges of all — it was against Widnes.

The game attracted an audience of 17,932 to see if Wigan could avenge their Isle of Man defeat or whether Widnes could upset the cup plans of their rivals once again.

A young man with a famous Rugby League name, however, helped to make sure that Widnes didn't pull off a repeat. Teenage fullback Sean Tyrer played a major part in Wigan's 14-10 victory by landing five goals, and that meant defeat for Widnes, the club where his dad, Colin, a former Wigan star and outstanding goalkicker, is assistant coach.

On to the final went Graham Lowe's men and a crowd of 19,167 turned up at Knowsley Road to see them take on Kevin Ashcroft's Salford side.

The final developed into an enthralling contest. Salford carried the game to Wigan from the start and at one stage were leading 3-0 with a penalty by Peter Brown and a drop

117. That's the style! . . . halfback Shaun Edwards darts through with plenty of support from Ellery Hanley.

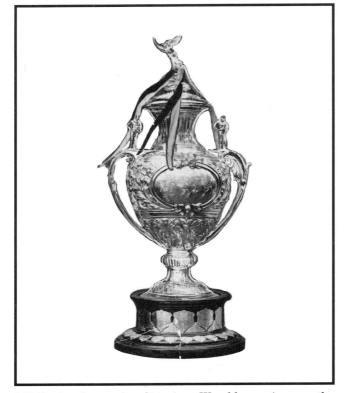

118. Rugby League's glittering Wembley prize — the Challenge Cup, which has been won by Wigan on ten occasions.

goal from Mick Worrall.

Back came Wigan! One of those superb Andy Gregory passes created a chance for Kevin Iro and the big New Zealand Test centre went storming in to score a try which he also improved. Iro added a penalty soon after and Wigan were beginning to get the edge, but early in the second half Salford forged ahead once more in a dramatic see-saw struggle.

Winger Tex Evans scored a good try, and a penalty by Brown made it 9-8 to Salford with their fans cheering themselves hoarse. Could they topple mighty Wigan, winners of the Trophy for the last three years?

The answer was not long in coming as Wigan struck back in dynamic style with a great Kiwi hat trick.

Three tries in eight minutes ended the Salford dream. Prop forward Adrian Shelford powered in for the first after a slick piece of passing by Andy Gregory. Substitute Dennis Betts set up the next try for Kevin Iro and centre Dean Bell completed the decisive spell when he kicked ahead and raced after the ball to touch down.

Kevin Iro added a goal and Wigan led 22-9 with only five minutes left to play but brave Salford battled on and earned two late tries to close the gap to 22-17 at the end of a magnificent final which reflected tremendous credit on both sides.

Wigan had done it again! They had carried off the Lancashire Cup for the fourth successive year and for a record twentieth time in all. Their team had been: Hampson, T Iro, K Iro, Bell, Lydon, Edwards, Gregory, Lucas, Dermott, Shelford, Platt, Goodway and Hanley.

Wigan were soon chasing yet another top award with the start of the John Player Trophy competition — and what a sensational start it turned out to be as a weakened Runcorn Highfield, hit by a players' dispute, came to Central Park and were beaten 92-2 with Kevin Iro scoring four tries and kicking nine goals.

There were much tougher tests ahead, however, and after a 26-16 win at Halifax in Round Two, Wigan had to travel to Humberside to face Hull Kingston Rovers at Craven Park. They came through with a 16-16 draw, but in the replay on the following Wednesday night with 12,896 people there to see the match Wigan scorched away with the game in a spectacular 30-0 triumph in which Joe Lydon landed five goals and Mark Preston scored two tries.

The semi-finals produced a clash with Bradford Northern at Headingley and the Wigan fans who travelled across the Pennines on that last Saturday before Christmas were rewarded with the best present of all — a place in the final. Wigan won 16-5 with their tries coming from Tony Iro, Joe Lydon and Ellery Hanley. Lydon also kicked two goals.

The festive holiday of 1988 was a good one for Wigan with a Boxing Day away win over St Helens by 18-11 in front of a crowd of 21,505, and a 26-10 home victory over Warrington on New Year's Day when 18,334 people turned up at Central Park for the derby clash.

It was the perfect run-up to the big date on 7 January at Burnden Park, home of Bolton Wanderers FC, where Wigan were to take on Widnes once again, this time to settle the destination of the John Player Trophy.

Rugby League supporters were there in strength — 20,709 of them — for what promised to be a classic final despite the wet and miserable weather. And what a classic it turned out to be with both sides locked in a tight and dramatic struggle which may not have produced high scores, but which lost nothing in excitement and entertainment.

It was a game dominated by the outstanding tackling of both sides, who went in at half-time with the scores at 6-6. Wigan surged ahead with a fine try when Shaun Edwards sent out a perfect pass to put Ged Byrne through, and Kevin Iro raced up in support to go over for the touch-down. Minutes later, however, Widnes had hit back when centre Darren Wright snapped up a neat interception and raced fifty yards for a try which Andy Currier improved.

Two penalties by Joe Lydon edged Wigan back in front but the game and the Trophy still hung desperately in the balance. Then a brilliant try by skipper Ellery Hanley crowned the victory for Wigan. Gregory put him through and the Wigan captain produced a spectacular run to the corner for a try which made sure that the John Player Trophy came back to Central Park for a record fourth occasion as Wigan won 12-6.

Wigan's team had lined up like this: Hampson, Bell, Kevin Iro, Lydon, Tony Iro, Byrne, Edwards, Shelford, Dermott, Wane, Betts, Potter and Hanley.

With two major trophies now proudly on display in the Central Park showcase, the thoughts of Wigan fans were again turning to the Silk Cut Challenge Cup and the prospects of another great Wembley final. But in their most optimistic dreams they could hardly have envisaged a more sensational finish to Wigan's Challenge Cup campaign in the 1988-89 season. If there was one side Wigan fans wanted to see a victory against at Wembley it was surely St Helens,

121. Congratulations . . . forward Andy Platt hugs Ellery Hanley in delight after the Wigan captain had touched down for yet another try.

their traditional rivals, who had twice sent them home beaten from the famous stadium in 1961 and 1966.

This was to be *the* year — but surely few Wigan fans can have foreseen how dramatic that final victory would be when the draw for the first round was made way back on that cold, early January morning.

Wigan drew a trip to Doncaster in round one and came through with their expected and decisive win. Joe Lydon scorched home for four tries as Wigan triumphed 38-6.

A much tougher task in Yorkshire awaited Wigan in the second round when they were paired against Bradford Northern at Odsal, but with tries by Shaun Edwards, Ged Byrne and hooker Nicky Kiss, plus two goals by Kevin Iro and a Joe Lydon drop goal, Wigan went forward into the last eight with a 17-4 success. Those great twin towers of Wembley must have been looming large on the horizon for the army of Wigan supporters as they travelled back across the Pennines that February Sunday evening, but Tuesday morning dawned with a third round draw which must have sent a shiver down more than a few Wigan supporters' spines!

Their Central Park heroes had been drawn away again — this time to Oldham to raise the spectre of Watersheddings two years earlier when a hoped for Grand Slam of every trophy by Wigan had been ruined by Oldham's surprise Cup knockout of the cherry and whites.

Wigan set about laying the ghost of Watersheddings in formidable style to go on to a well-earned 12-4 win with tries by Shaun Edwards and Kevin Iro. Once again, Joe Lydon had his name on the score sheet, this time with two goals.

But the score by Lydon which really hit the sporting headlines and captured the imagination of millions of people who saw the achievement on TV or at Maine Road was yet to come! Wigan went into the last four knowing that they would be facing derby opponents at Wembley on 29 April if they got through. The strength of the Rugby League game in the local area was again emphasised as Wigan, Warrington, St Helens and Widnes provided the teams for the semi-finals of the Silk Cut Challenge Cup.

It would be Lancashire's day at Wembley! At least that's how many local Rugby League folk viewed the situation, even though changed boundaries now meant that two of the last four were Cheshire clubs, with one from Merseyside and the other — Wigan — now in Greater Manchester.

Whatever their new counties, the fans at Wembley still sang *Lassie from Lancashire* in resounding voice when they filled the Wembley terraces that April Saturday!

Wigan were paired with their great rivals Warrington for the semis, but first they played host at Central Park to the other semi-final. More than 17,000 spectators poured into the ground to see a thrilling struggle between the favourites Widnes and Alex Murphy's St Helens side.

St Helens won 16-14 in a breathtaking finish which also left Wigan supporters now eagerly anticipating the chance of that long-awaited Wembley 'return' against their Knowsley Road rivals.

First, though, a tough semi-final hurdle against Warrington had to be surmounted at Maine Road. The Wires set Wigan a formidable task in a game dominated by some fine tackling from both sides, but also involving some exhilarating attacking play.

It was another classic semi-final, played before an

122. Wigan captain Ellery Hanley whose brilliant display at Wembley in the runaway win against St Helens earned him the Lance Todd Award as the outstanding player of the final. The Great Britain skipper is the seventh Wigan player to join the famous Lance Todd roll of honour, following in the footsteps of Cec Mountford (1951), Rees Thomas (1958), Brian McTigue (1959), Ray Ashby (1965), Brett Kenny (1985) and Andy Gregory (1988).

audience of 26,529 which once more provided a marvellous advertisement for the game of Rugby League football. Joe Lydon scored a vital first try and kept Wigan well in the picture with his goalkicking, but it was a towering drop goal from all of sixty yards out that seized everyone's imagination. It also sent just about everyone delving through the record books in the succeeding days to try to discover if it was, in fact, the longest drop goal in Rugby League history. There can be no doubt that it was one of the most spectacular — and one of the most important.

Lydon's cool composure, plus the power and accuracy of his kicking, had produced a drop goal which would still be a big discussion point whenever Rugby League was the topic of conversation, long after the result of that dramatic semi-final had been reduced to a statistic in the record books.

Wigan went on to win 13-6 with Ellery Hanley sparking off a great try by Shaun Edwards in the closing stages to crown the Wigan success. It was Edwards' third try of the cup run — and as he touched down the Wembley chants were already sounding out strong and clear from the powerful Wigan contingent around the Maine Road ground.

123. Wembley action . . . Andy Platt gets to grips with Saints Aussie loose forward Paul Vautin.

Hopes of a trophy Grand Slam were riding high again, but it was to be a disappointment for Wigan in the Premiership when they were beaten by Saints, and also in the Stones Bitter Championship where Widnes pipped them in the final match in a breathtaking finish to the title race after a great 16-match winning run by Wigan.

But on the last Saturday of April the streets of London were alive to Northern accents once again as Wigan and St Helens returned to face each other against the magnificent backcloth of Wembley Stadium for the first time since 1966.

The stage was set for a classic final. Could Wigan prevent Saints from making it a hat trick against them and retain the trophy they had won in such fine style just twelve months earlier, or would Alex Murphy's men repeat the successes of their predecessors in the Sixties?

The prospects were intriguing as the fans streamed in to fill up the stadium to its new capacity figure of 77,500.

Saints had won the toss to wear their traditional red and white colours. Wigan fans had to put away the 1988 cherry and white Wembley colours and dress themselves up in the less familiar blue and white.

The highly entertaining schoolboy curtain-raiser match brought the first Wigan success of the day as the town's under-11s team defeated Castleford boys 6-0.

When Wigan and Saints players entered the arena to a roar fit to raise the roof, it must have been a most poignant moment for one player in particular.

Wigan fullback Steve Hampson was at last treading that famous turf as a Cup finalist after a sequence of wretched luck over injuries which had denied him the chance of appearing in three previous finals. When Wigan faced Widnes at Wembley in 1984 the unlucky Hampson had to sit out the match with a broken leg. Twelve months later a broken arm ended his Wembley dream when Wigan

124. The line is in sight . . . Kevin Iro surges forward with Shane Cooper trying to stop him.

125. Wigan's international fullback Steve Hampson for whom the Wembley win against St Helens in May 1989 had extra special significance. Three times the unlucky Hampson missed out on Wembley finals because of wretched luck over injuries. But the talented fullback kept coming back in great style and eventually savoured the magic atmosphere of Wembley. And to complete a great day he rounded off Wigan's win over Saints with a fine try.

took on Hull, and in 1988 another injury set-back prevented him from playing in the Cup final against Halifax.

The feel of that Wembley turf must have been particularly good to the young fullback as he stepped out with his team-mates — and it was an afternoon that was to get better and better all the time for Wigan and their supporters.

The match was just two minutes old when Wigan struck for their first try to send shock waves around the St Helens terraces and set the Wigan fans leaping for joy. Skipper Ellery Hanley burst through on a fine run and sent the powerful New Zealand Test centre Kevin Iro driving for the line in a great piece of finishing for a marvellous opening try.

St Helens struggled to get their attacking game together, dropping too many passes and generally proving to be disappointing, but Wigan went on to stamp their authority on the final with a performance which in my opinion was nothing short of world class. Certainly the next try by Hanley was one of the best ever seen at Wembley as he beat five defenders with a sensational piece of running to touch down behind the posts. Joe Lydon tacked on the goal and

Wigan were leading 12-0 after 25 minutes, and that's how it stayed up to half-time.

The interval buzz around the ground was full of anticipation . . . could Saints make a dramatic second-half comeback or would Wigan drive home their advantage to take the Trophy?

The answers were not long in coming. After three minutes Andy Gregory chipped over a neat drop goal. Four minutes later Kevin Iro was over for his second try after a superb combined move full of good handling and strong support play at speed. It was Iro's fourth Wembley try in two years — a record.

Wigan had their opponents on the rack now and it was Shaun Edwards who next carved the Saints' defence wide open with a magnificent run down the middle. Halfback partner Andy Gregory swept up in support to complete another great try which Joe Lydon improved. Wigan were leading 23-0 and the big issue in question had suddenly become whether Saints could get some points on the Wembley scoreboard or end up as the first side to be nilled at Wembley since 1951.

Sadly, for Saints, that was how it did finish. The final word came from Wigan with the perfect crowning touch to a memorable day for Steve Hampson as he stormed through from fullback with a tremendous left wing run to score the final try six minutes from time.

Wigan had won 27-0 in one of the most one-sided finals for years. Ellery Hanley led his team-mates up to the Royal Box to receive the Silk Cut Challenge Cup from Lord Whitelaw accompanied by a mighty roar from the Wigan fans. They cheered themselves hoarse as the Wigan heroes took the lap of honour.

The teams had lined up like this: for St Helens, Connolly, O'Connor, Veivers, Loughlin, Quirk, Cooper, Holding, Burke, Groves, Forber, Dwyer, Haggerty and Vautin; subs: Bloor and Evans. For Wigan, Hampson, T Iro, K Iro, Bell, Lydon, Edwards, Gregory, Lucas, Kiss, Shelford, Platt, Potter and Hanley; subs: Betts and Goodway.

Wigan folk again turned out in their thousands when Graham Lowe and his men returned to Wigan with the trophy to a rousing homecoming.

The end of the season, however, was tinged with sadness with the news that Graham Lowe would be leaving for Australia after the summer promotion game against Warrington in Milwaukee, USA.

The highly popular New Zealander had won a special place in the hearts of every Wigan supporter. His magnificent record during a three-season period included no fewer than ten major trophies and honours, including, of course, the Big One — the Challenge Cup — on two occasions.

In the new season, 1989-90, Wigan will be aiming to achieve a momentous hat trick by becoming the first club in the history of Rugby League football to win the Trophy in three successive years.

They are moving forward into a new and exciting decade which promises so much for them and Rugby League in general, on the very crest of a wave of success. What better way to step into the Nineties!

That Wigan success story looks set to run and run . . .

126. Bang on target! . . . The brilliant goal-kicking of Joe Lydon has been a vital factor for Wigan on many occasions. Here he steers home another goal.

127. A typical attacking burst from Andy Gregory.

128. More big match action as Shaun Edwards and Andy Gregory show their paces.

129. Wembley action . . . no way through this time for Wigan.

130. In the thick of the action . . . Wigan try to launch another raid but Saints look to have this one covered.

131. Away he goes! . . . Ellery Hanley in another exciting break for the line.

132. *top left:* Andy Gregory, another of Wigan's international stars who was among the try-scorers at Wembley. Gregory is also a winner of the Lance Todd Trophy from the Wembley victory against Halifax in 1988. He now has no fewer than five Wembley appearances to his credit!

133. *top right:* Andy Platt, one of Wigan's major signings of the 1988-89 season, joining the Central Park club from St Helens for a record fee for a forward. He played for Saints at Wembley against Halifax in 1987.

134. *left:* Powerful New Zealand Test centre Kevin Iro who scored the first try of the Wembley triumph against St Helens. He went on to score another — making it a Wembley record four in two finals.

135. Wide-angled view of the action as Tony Iro speeds through.
136. Forward power . . . front row man Brian Case in action.

137. *top left:* Hooker Nicky Kiss, who has earned a winner's medal in three Wembley finals with Wigan against Hull in 1985, Halifax in 1988 and St Helens in 1989.

138. *top right:* New Zealand threequarter Dean Bell, another of Wigan's strong international contingent. Bell has been capped no fewer than 21 times for his country and has also captained the Kiwi Test side.

139. *left:* Prop forward Ian Lucas, a product of the highly successful Wigan Colts side, who has won Colts and under-21 international honours. Ian gained his first major winner's medal in the Grunhalle Lancashire Cup victory over Salford in October 1988 and rounded off an excellent season with a Wembley winner's medal. He is one of the best young forwards in the Rugby League game.

140. Down he goes. No way through here against a strong Wigan defence.
141. Heroes of '89. The Wigan squad line up for the photographers.

142. Kevin Iro takes on the defence.

143. New Zealand Test forward Graeme West drives into the attack.

144. Singing in the rain! Andy Gregory shares a joke with photographers.

145. We've done it! . . . Andy Gregory and Joe Lydon show their delight after the Cup final victory over Saints.

146. Great Britain star Andy Gregory.

147. Happy Hampson . . . the Wigan fullback scorches over to score a try in the 1989 Wembley final.

148. The moment of victory. A hug and a handshake for coach Graham Lowe on the Wembley bench after the 1989 Cup triumph against St Helens.
149. Hail the heroes . . . the Wigan fans go wild with delight as they salute their players who have just received the Silk Cut Challenge Cup in the 1989 final.

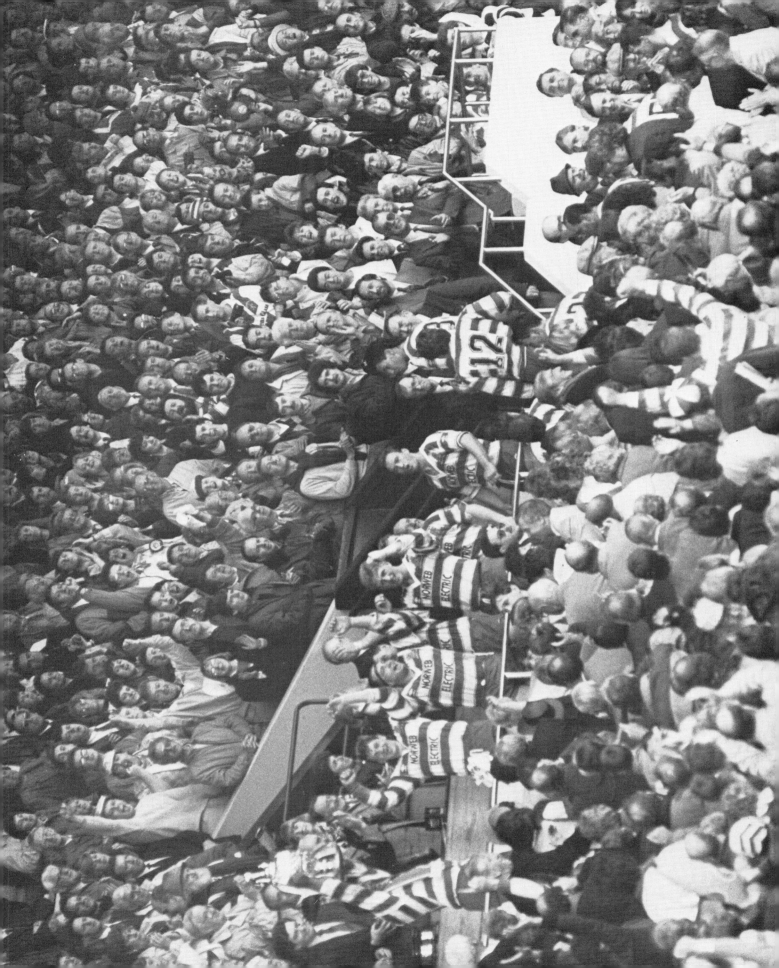

150. Shaun Edwards speeds through.

151. Shaun Edwards concentrates as he prepares to make a tackle.

152. Salute to the heroes! Wigan supporters applaud and cheer their team as Ellery Hanley lifts the Silk Cut Challenge Cup aloft after the dramatic Wembley win against St Helens which halted Saints' bid for a hat trick of Wembley triumphs against their traditional rivals.

153. Here we go . . . Wigan players display the Cup to their Wembley supporters.

154. It's ours! . . . Coach Graham Lowe and captain Ellery Hanley on the Wembley lap of honour, 1989.

155. Pride and joy . . . the Central Park heroes celebrate the 1989 victory against Saints.

156. Another trophy for Central Park . . . Ellery Hanley proudly holds the Silk Cut Challenge Cup after the runaway victory against St Helens.

157. Andy Gregory darts through.

159. Ellery Hanley in the semi-final action.

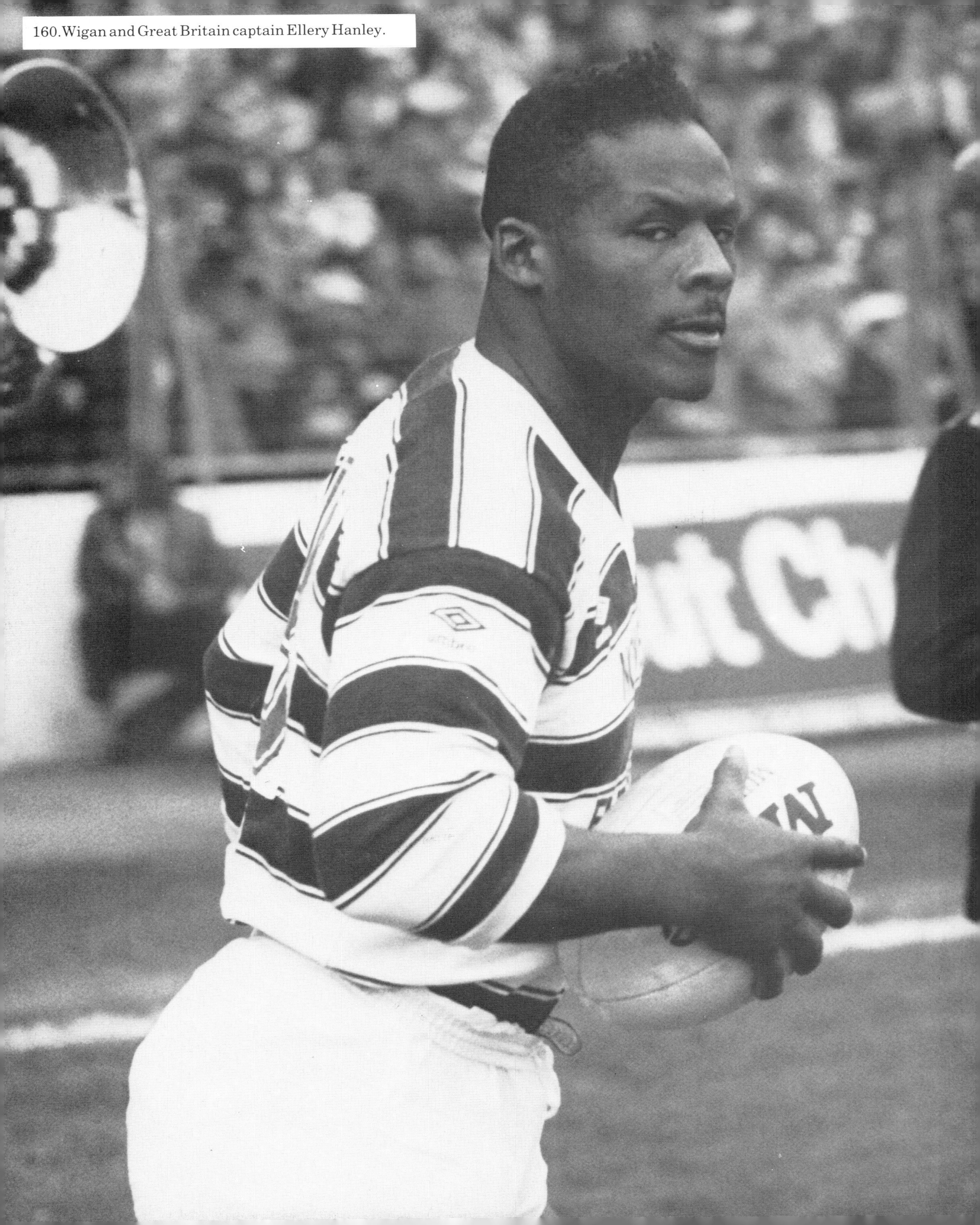

160. Wigan and Great Britain captain Ellery Hanley.

161. Andy Platt and Adrian Shelford team up to halt a Warrington semi-final attack.

163. Andy Platt shows his paces.

164. Dean Bell tries to force a way through.

165. Adrian Shelford dashes through.

166. Tony Iro takes on the defence.

167. Tony Iro in action at Maine Road.

168. Ellery Hanley puts the pressure on Warrington.

169. Crowning touch! Andy Goodway and Ian Lucas lift the Challenge Cup high as they enjoy the Wembley lap of honour with coach Graham Lowe and skipper Ellery Hanley after the triumph over St Helens. Nicky Kiss is on the left of the picture.

170. Wembley triumph....Parading the Cup after the victory over St Helens